Strategic HRM for Sustainable Healthcare: Navigating the Path to Excellence

DR. RUCHI SINGH MAURYA

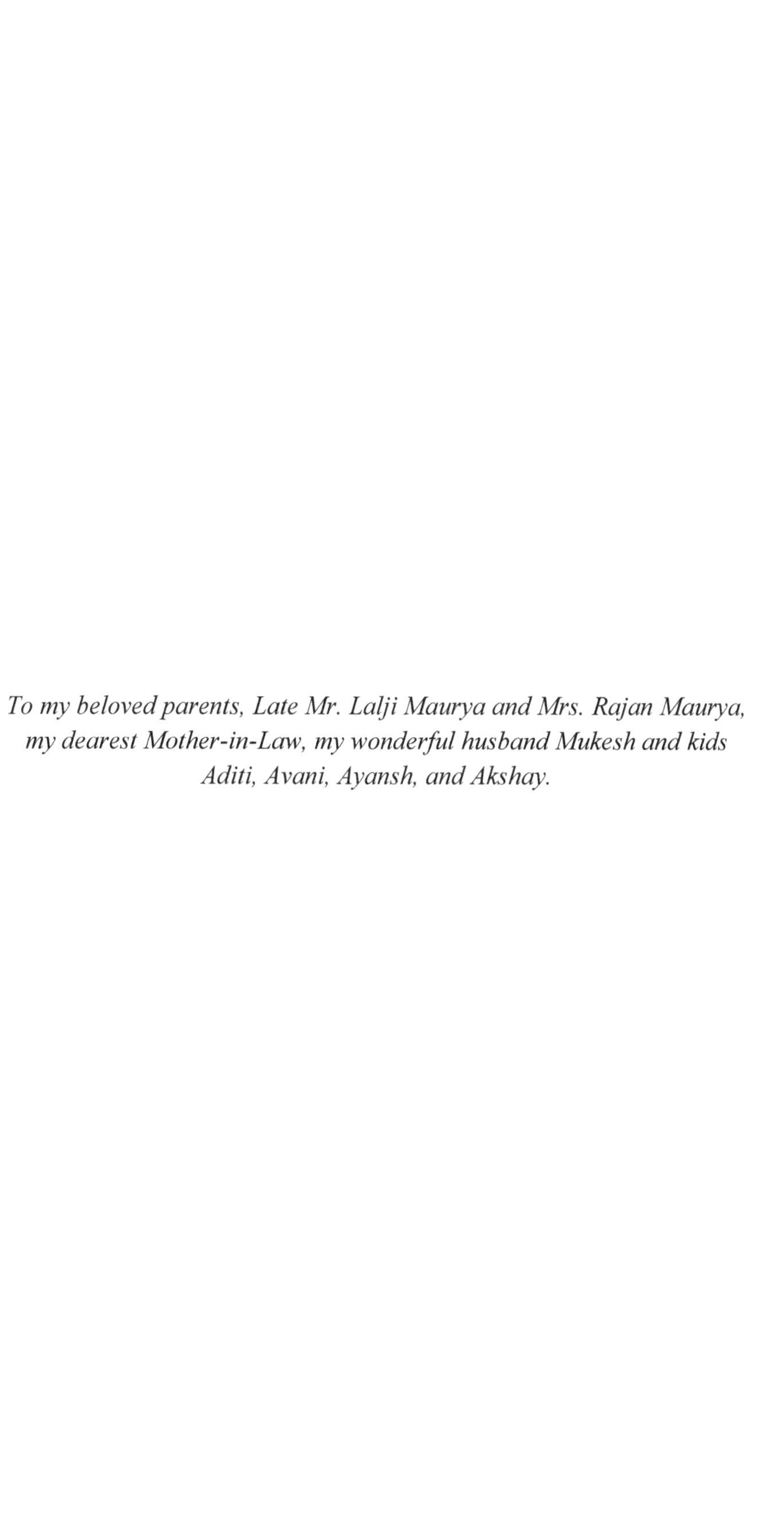

To my beloved parents, Late Mr. Lalji Maurya and Mrs. Rajan Maurya, my dearest Mother-in-Law, my wonderful husband Mukesh and kids Aditi, Avani, Ayansh, and Akshay.

Contents

Preface

Welcome to "Strategic HRM for Sustainable Healthcare: Navigating the Path to Excellence." As the author of this book, I am delighted to take you on a journey exploring the intersection of strategic human resource management (HRM) and sustainability within the dynamic realm of healthcare organizations.

This endeavor began as a research, a humble exploration into the role of high-performance HR practices in advancing sustainability within healthcare. The more I delved into the subject, the more I realized the profound impact that strategic HRM could have on shaping the future of healthcare excellence. This realization fueled my desire to expand the discussion and share the insights gained through meticulous research and thoughtful analysis.

Why "Strategic HRM for Sustainable Healthcare"?

In the pages that follow, you will find a synthesis of my findings, reflections, and aspirations for a sustainable healthcare landscape. The title encapsulates the essence of the book — a focus on the strategic application of human resource management principles in fostering sustainability within healthcare organizations by enhancing employee retention. It is my belief that a strategic approach to HRM is not merely a component but a catalyst for excellence in healthcare.

What to Expect:

Exploration of High Performance HR Practices: Delve into the mutually reinforcing bundle of HR practices and their relevance in the healthcare context. Understand how they can be a transformative force in organizational dynamics.

Primary Data based Results and Discussions: Unveiling insights derived from original research, this segment unveils the direct outcomes of my primary data investigation. By presenting data-driven results, I aim to illuminate the specific impact of high-performance HR practices on sustainable healthcare within organizational settings. Through focused discussions, we navigate the intricacies of our findings, offering readers a firsthand look into the empirical foundations that underpin the transformative potential of strategic HRM in the healthcare landscape.

Guidance for Practitioners: This book is not just for academics; it is a practical guide for HR professionals, healthcare leaders, and anyone passionate about creating sustainable healthcare environments. Practical insights and actionable strategies await those ready to embark on this transformative journey.

I extend my heartfelt gratitude to **Dr. Shine David** whose support and guidance have enriched this work. His contribution has been invaluable, and I am deeply appreciative of his commitment to advancing my knowledge in research field.

As you embark on this exploration of strategic HRM and sustainability in healthcare, I invite you to engage with the material, reflect on its implications, and envision a future where excellence and sustainability go hand in hand. I hope this book sparks meaningful conversations, inspires positive change, and contributes to the ongoing dialogue on shaping the future of healthcare.

Thank you for joining me on this journey!

Dr. Ruchi Singh Maurya

1. Strategic HRM

1.1 Introduction

Before we jump into this chapter, let me ask you a question: Would a company trying to save money with a cost-cutting strategy hire people the same way as a company trying to stand out in the market? Probably not. The first company would pick hiring methods that save money, while the second would focus on finding talent that helps it stand out. This is where Human Resource Management (HRM) connects with strategy, forming what we call Strategic HRM. It's all about making sure HR practices match up with what the company is trying to achieve, whether it's saving money or standing out in the market.

Let's explore some more examples showing how different organizational strategies might influence their training practices:

- **Technology Adoption Company:** Consider a tech-forward company with a strategy focused on staying ahead in technology adoption. In this case, their training practices would likely emphasize continuous learning and upskilling in the latest technological advancements. Employees might attend regular workshops and receive online courses to stay updated in a rapidly evolving tech landscape. This contrasts with a company pursuing cost reduction, which might opt for more streamlined and cost-effective training methods.

- **Quality and Excellence-Oriented Manufacturer:** Imagine a manufacturing company committed to delivering top-notch quality and excellence in its products. Their training practices would likely involve rigorous quality control and specialized skills development to maintain high standards. On the contrary, a company with a cost-cutting strategy might focus on basic training to ensure efficiency in processes without extensive specialization.

- **Customer-Centric Service Provider:** Picture a service-oriented business aiming for exceptional customer service. Their training practices might prioritize soft skills development, such as effective communication and problem-solving, to enhance the customer experience. Conversely, a company pursuing rapid expansion might opt for more streamlined training practices to quickly onboard new employees and enter new markets.

- **Environmentally Conscious Organization:** Consider an organization with a strong commitment to environmental sustainability. Their training practices might include programs educating employees on eco-friendly practices and incorporating sustainability into daily operations. This differs from a company focused on short-term profitability, which might prioritize cost-effective and quick training methods.

These examples illustrate how diverse organizational strategies can shape training practices, emphasizing the need for alignment between training and the overarching goals of the company.

I hope that you now grasp the significance of aligning HR policies and practices with the strategic objectives of the organization. Let's reconsider organizations that lack this alignment, employing analogous HR practices, and contemplate the repercussions of such misalignment. I hope you've come up with brilliant examples. Allow me to share one as well. Envision a company with a primary focus on cost-cutting as its strategic objective. Now, if its HR policies do not align with this goal, and instead emphasize hiring practices geared towards premium skill acquisition without cost considerations, it could lead to increased expenses. The misalignment between HR practices and the organization's strategic objective may result in financial inefficiencies, hindering the company's ability to achieve its overarching goal of cost reduction. This example highlights how the lack of synchronization between HR strategies and organizational objectives can impede overall success.

1.2 Definition of Strategic Human Resource Management

"Strategic Human Resource Management integrates human resource management goals and objectives with information on external opportunities and threats, and the organization's own strengths and weaknesses. The aim of strategic human resource management is to improve business performance and develop an organizational culture that fosters innovation and flexibility."

- **Michael Armstrong**

"Strategic Human Resource Management involves the formulation and implementation of HRM systems and practices that produce the employee competencies and behaviors the company needs to achieve its strategic aims."

- **Jeffrey A. Mello**

These definitions capture the essence of Strategic HRM, emphasizing the integration of HRM goals with broader organizational strategies to enhance business performance and achieve strategic aims. Exploring these books further can provide a comprehensive understanding of the principles, practices, and real-world applications of strategic human resource management.

1.3 Why it is important to integrate HR practices to Organizational Strategic Objectives?

Imagine a company is like a puzzle, and each piece of the puzzle is a different aspect of the business – like people, money, and technology. Integrating human resource (HR) practices means making sure that these pieces fit together well with the company's big plans and goals.

Here's why this is important:

i   **Solving Tricky Problems:** When all the pieces of the puzzle work together, it helps the company solve difficult problems. For example, if a company wants to grow, it needs to make sure it has the right people, enough money, and the latest technology. Integrating HR practices helps in finding solutions for such complex issues.

ii **Considering Everything Important:** Integrating means thinking about all the important things – the people in the company (human resources), the money it has, and the technology it uses. It's like making sure everyone's ideas and needs are taken into account when deciding what the company should achieve and how it should do it.

iii **Putting Plans into Action:** Through integration, companies not only make plans but also make sure those plans happen. This involves thinking about the individuals who make up the company and creating rules and ways of doing things that everyone follows.

iv **Balancing Needs:** Integrating human resources with the big plans of the company ensures that neither side (strategic plans or human resources) becomes less important. It's like having a balance – the company's big goals are crucial, but so are the people who work there. Both contribute to the company's success.

So, integrating HR practices with organizational goals is like making sure all the puzzle pieces fit well together to create a successful and balanced picture for the company.

1.4 How Human Resource Management (HRM) has evolved into what we now recognize as Strategic Human Resource Management (SHRM).

In the dynamic landscape of modern organizations, Human Resource Management (HRM) has evolved beyond traditional administrative functions to become a critical strategic component. It was the late 20th century and the early 21st century when HRM has entered Strategic HRM era. During this period, Human Resource Management underwent a transformation, assuming the role of a strategic ally within organizations. Its emphasis transitioned from a support function to a crucial element actively shaping the overarching business strategy.

1.4.1 Personnel Management to HRM to SHRM: A Transition

The evolution from Personnel Management (PM) to Human Resource Management (HRM) and subsequently to Strategic Human Resource Management (SHRM) represents a paradigm shift in the way organizations perceive and manage their workforce. The transition reflects a maturation of the HR function from a transactional and administrative role to a strategic and integral part of organizational success. It underscores the growing recognition of the importance of human capital in achieving sustained competitive advantage.

Let's explore each stage of this transition:

(i) Personnel Management (PM): Personnel Management (PM) is a historical approach that originated in the early 20th century, marked by a distinct administrative focus. During this period, organizations primarily viewed their workforce as a collection of individual employees, and the main responsibilities of personnel management were centered around routine tasks.

Focus: Personnel Management's central focus was on administrative duties that included tasks like payroll processing, tracking attendance, and ensuring adherence to labor laws. The approach was largely reactive, addressing immediate needs and maintaining records related to employee activities.

Relationship: In the realm of personnel management, the relationship between employees and the organization was often characterized as contractual. Employees were seen as individual entities, and the organizational structure tended to be hierarchical. Decisions flowed from the top down, reflecting an authoritative approach where directives were issued, and compliance was expected.

Objectives: The primary objectives of personnel management were clear-cut and limited to maintaining compliance with employment laws, keeping accurate records, and handling routine personnel tasks efficiently. The goal was to establish order and ensure that the organization met legal requirements concerning its workforce.

In essence, Personnel Management during this era can be likened to a bureaucratic system with a primary focus on paperwork, legalities, and administrative efficiency. The approach was essential for ensuring basic organizational operations but lacked a more strategic, forward-looking perspective that could contribute to long-term organizational success.

(ii) Human Resource Management (HRM):

Focus: Human Resource Management (HRM) emerged as a transformative approach in the latter half of the 20th century, departing from the administrative confines of Personnel Management. Unlike its predecessor, HRM adopted a more expansive and strategic focus, recognizing employees not merely as individuals but as valuable assets critical to organizational success.

Relationship: In contrast to the contractual and authoritative nature of personnel management, HRM witnessed a paradigm shift in the perception of employees. They were now considered integral resources contributing to the organization's overall success. The HR function transitioned into a more strategic role, actively participating in organizational decision-making processes.

Objectives: HRM broadened its objectives beyond the routine administrative tasks of its predecessor. It embraced a holistic approach that included talent acquisition, training and development, performance management, and employee engagement. The primary goal of HRM was to enhance organizational performance through the effective management and development of its human capital.

This shift marked a departure from the traditional view of HR as merely handling paperwork and enforcing compliance. Instead, HRM aimed to align its practices with the overarching goals of the organization, acknowledging the critical role employees play in achieving sustained success. The emphasis on strategic decision-making, talent development, and employee engagement distinguished HRM as a dynamic and integral function within modern organizations.

(iii) Strategic Human Resource Management (SHRM):

Focus: Think of SHRM like making a puzzle. Each piece of the puzzle represents a person in the company. SHRM is about making sure these puzzle pieces (people or human resources) fit perfectly with the overall picture, or plan, of the company. It's not just about having people work; it's about making sure they work in a way that helps the company succeed in its big plans.

Relationship: In SHRM, employees are not seen only as workers; they're considered important partners in the company's success. It's like playing on a sports team where every player is crucial to winning. In SHRM, the Human Resources (HR) department works closely with the leaders of the company. They're like teammates; making decisions together to help the whole team (company) reach its goals.

Objectives: SHRM thinks about the future and plans for the long term. It's not just about getting through the day but making sure everyone is prepared for what's coming next. This involves making sure the right people are doing the right jobs, helping each person grow and get better, and creating a positive and happy work environment. It's like preparing for a big game where everyone knows their role, practices to get better, and supports each other to win.

In simple terms, SHRM is like being part of a well-organized team where everyone has an important role to play, and they work together to make sure the team wins in the long run. It's about making the best use of everyone's skills and making sure everyone is happy and motivated to contribute to the success of the whole organization.

Key Transitions and Characteristics:

- **Focus on Strategy:** The transition from PM to HRM and then to SHRM involves a progressive shift from a primarily administrative focus to a strategic focus, where HR practices are tightly linked to organizational goals.

- **Employee Relationship:** The relationship between the organization and its employees evolves from a contractual and transactional nature to a more collaborative and strategic partnership.

- **Role of HR:** In PM, HR was seen as an administrative function, while in HRM, it evolved into a more strategic partner. In SHRM, HR plays a crucial role in shaping and executing organizational strategy.

- **Integration with Business Strategy:** SHRM is characterized by the seamless integration of HR practices with the overall business strategy. This integration ensures that HR decisions and initiatives contribute directly to achieving the organization's strategic objectives.

- **Continuous Learning and Adaptation:** SHRM recognizes the dynamic nature of the business environment. HR professionals in this stage must continuously learn, adapt, and align HR practices with changing organizational needs.

1.4.2 Difference between HRM and strategic HRM

Aspect	Human Resource Management	Strategic Human Resource Management
Scope	Primarily focuses on day-to-day HR functions, administrative tasks, and compliance.	Encompasses a broader scope, integrating HR practices with organizational strategy.

Goals and Objectives	Aims to manage and optimize workforce efficiently, ensuring HR processes run smoothly.	Aligns HR goals and objectives with overall organizational objectives and strategies.
Time Horizon	Often short-term and reactive, addressing immediate HR needs.	Long-term and proactive, anticipating future challenges and aligning with organizational goals.
Integration with Strategy	Generally seen as a support function with limited integration into overall business strategy.	Actively participates in shaping and executing organizational strategy, influencing business decisions.
Focus on Employees	Emphasizes employee relations, HR policies, and day-to-day operations.	Focuses not only on employees but also on talent management, development, and creating a positive workplace culture.
Decision-making Role	More administrative and transactional in decision-making.	A strategic partner involved in strategic decision-making, contributing insights on workforce planning, talent acquisition, and development.

1.4.3 Example

Aspect	Human Resource Management	Strategic Human Resource Management
Performance Evaluation	***Periodic Performance Appraisal:*** In the HRM context, performance appraisal typically involves setting predefined performance	***Strategic Performance Management:Strategic*** Performance Management within SHRM integrates performance appraisal with broader

	goals, conducting annual or semi-annual reviews, and providing feedback to employees. The primary goal is to evaluate individual performance, identify areas for improvement, and make decisions related to compensation and promotions based on historical performance data.	organizational goals. Instead of focusing solely on historical performance, SHRM emphasizes ongoing feedback, goal alignment, and professional development. The process may include regular check-ins, collaborative goal-setting, and a focus on skills development to ensure that employees' performance contributes directly to achieving strategic objectives.
Training and Development	***Reactive Training for Immediate Needs:*** HRM's approach to training and development involves identifying specific skill deficiencies or compliance requirements and implementing training sessions accordingly. The focus is on providing employees with the necessary knowledge and skills to perform their current roles effectively. While these programs may be valuable for individual skill	***Proactive and Strategic Learning and Development:*** SHRM recognizes learning and development as integral components of organizational success. Strategic programs may involve identifying future skill needs, implementing leadership development initiatives, and fostering a learning culture that adapts to industry trends. The emphasis is on equipping employees with the skills needed not just for their current roles but

	enhancement, they may not always align with long-term organizational strategies.	also for future challenges, contributing to the organization's long-term competitiveness.

In the realm of Strategic Human Resource Management (SHRM), two indispensable tools—Environmental Scanning and SWOT Analysis—serve as the guiding compass for HR professionals to navigate the dynamic business landscape and steer their organizations towards sustained success.

1.5 Environmental Scanning: A Proactive Vision

Environmental scanning is analogous to equipping HR with binoculars, allowing them to focus on the external world, identifying potential opportunities and threats that could influence HR strategies. Consider a tech company observing the growing trend of remote work due to digital communication advancements. By scanning this shift, the HR team can proactively introduce flexible work policies, attracting a wider talent pool and enhancing employee satisfaction. Similarly, legislative changes promoting diversity and inclusion require the HR department to adjust practices, implement diversity training, and foster an inclusive workplace culture, turning compliance into an opportunity for building a more diverse and innovative workforce.

1.5.1 SWOT Analysis: A Comprehensive HR Health Check-up

In the SHRM toolkit, SWOT analysis acts as a comprehensive HR health check-up. Imagine a retail company conducting a SWOT analysis, revealing a highly motivated and customer-focused sales team as strength. HR can leverage this by investing in ongoing training programs to enhance product knowledge and customer service skills. Conversely, identifying a weakness in outdated point-of-sale systems prompts HR to advocate for technology upgrades, enhancing efficiency.

Now, consider an external opportunity for global talent acquisition due to remote work trends. A SWOT analysis aids HR in aligning internal strengths, like a robust onboarding process, to seamlessly attract and integrate international talent. Simultaneously, it highlights threats such as intense competition for skilled professionals, prompting HR to implement retention strategies and innovative employee development programs.

1.5.2 Integration into Strategic HRM: Steering the Ship

The synergy of environmental scanning and SWOT analysis forms the dynamic duo of Strategic HRM. For scholars seeking real-world applications, envision steering a ship. Environmental scanning helps HR navigate through changing waters, while SWOT analysis ensures the ship is well-equipped and the crew is ready to face challenges and capitalize on opportunities. This proactive, adaptive approach aligns HR practices with broader organizational goals, ensuring sustained success in the competitive business landscape.

1.5.3 SWOT Analysis: Assessing HR Capabilities

Now, let's apply the concepts to a fictional company, Aditi Innovations Co., through a SWOT analysis for its HR department:

Strengths:

- *Highly Skilled Workforce:* Boasting cutting-edge skills in technology development.

- *Proactive Employee Engagement Initiatives:* Successful initiatives fostering a positive workplace culture.

- *Strategic Recruitment Practices:* A history of attracting top talent through innovative recruitment strategies.

Weaknesses:

- *Outdated HR Technology:* Relying on outdated systems, hindering efficiency.

- *Limited Diversity and Inclusion Programs:* A need for enhanced initiatives.

- *Communication Gaps:* Occasional gaps affecting the effectiveness of HR initiatives.

Opportunities:

- *Global Talent Acquisition:* Tapping into a global talent pool through remote work trends.

- *Technological Advancements in HR:* Streamlining processes with modern HR technology.

- *Strategic Workforce Planning:* Leveraging data analytics for effective planning.

Threats:

- *Talent Competition:* Intense industry competition impacting skilled professional retention.

- *Changing Employment Laws:* Evolving regulations requiring adjustments to HR policies.

- *Economic Downturn:* Potential impact on the budget for HR initiatives and training programs.

Integration into Strategic HRM: Using this SWOT analysis, Aditi Innovations Co.'s HR department can formulate strategies leveraging strengths, addressing weaknesses, seizing opportunities, and mitigating threats. Aligning global talent acquisition opportunities with strategic recruitment practices and addressing the weakness of outdated technology ensures that HR practices contribute strategically to the organization's advancement. This integrated approach reflects the proactive and adaptive nature of Strategic HRM, aligning HR initiatives with broader organizational goals for sustained success.

2. High Performance HR Practices

In the last chapter, we explored the concept of strategic HRM and distinguished it from the broader HRM discipline. Now, let's delve into the most influential tool of strategic HRM: High-Performance HR Practices. What sets these apart from conventional HR practices? Let's find out.

Opening Vignette

Picture Radha, a skilled professional maneuvering through the corporate world in bustling Mumbai. In the heart of Human Resource Management, Radha finds herself at a crossroads – the traditional route of HR practices or the fascinating territory of High-Performance HR Practices.

As she steps into this journey, the office corridors hum with tales of transformation. People speak of practices that go beyond the usual, not just promising efficiency but weaving a profound impact on the entire organizational fabric.

In this story of corporate exploration, we'll uncover the mysteries of High-Performance HR Practices – the silent architects shaping the future of the workforce in Radha's workplace. What sets them apart from the usual methods? Join Radha as she unravels the power of strategic HRM, opening a new chapter in the evolution of human resources.

2.1 Unveiling the Essence of High-Performance HR Practices

High-Performance HR Practices constitute a strategic framework implemented by HR professionals to optimize organizational performance. In contrast to conventional methods, these practices function cohesively, with each element complementing and reinforcing the others. The combined effect transcends the limitations of individual practices, propelling overall organizational performance to unprecedented heights. To illustrate this synergy, let's consider a practical example:

Suppose Radha's company decides to adopt a cost reduction strategy. As part of this initiative, they opt to hire MBA holders instead of IITians and decide to conduct comprehensive training programs to equip these new hires with the necessary knowledge and skills. In this scenario, the training practices complement and enhance the effectiveness of the hiring practices. This synergy ensures that the newly recruited employees, despite their different academic backgrounds, are brought up to the desired level of proficiency through targeted training.

Similarly, if compensation practices are aligned and complementary, the collective impact of hiring, training, and compensation practices becomes significantly more potent compared to if these three practices were unrelated, non-complementary, and operated in isolation. The interconnectedness and mutual support among these practices creates a multiplier effect, where the whole becomes greater than the sum of its parts.

In essence, the integration of High-Performance HR Practices transforms individual HR components into a unified force, working in tandem to achieve overarching organizational goals. The example of Radha's company illustrates how the harmonious interplay of hiring, training, and compensation practices can elevate the effectiveness of each element, leading to a more resilient and high-performing organization. This holistic approach is the key to navigating the complexities of the modern business landscape and achieving sustained success.

2.2 Definition of High Performance HR Practices

"High-Performance Work Practices are practices that lead to superior performance by the workforce. These practices are associated with higher levels of employee skills and abilities, enhanced motivation and commitment, and better retention of the talented workforce."

-   (Becker, 1998)

2.3 Characteristics of High Performance HR Practices

High-Performance Human Resource Practices (HPHRPs) exhibit several key characteristics that contribute to their effectiveness in enhancing organizational performance:

i Interconnected:

HPHRPs are intricately linked, forming a cohesive system where each practice influences and complements the others. This interconnectedness ensures that the overall human resource strategy aligns seamlessly with organizational goals.

ii Inter-related:

These practices are interdependent, with each one relying on the successful implementation of others. For instance, effective recruitment is contingent on the availability of well-designed training programs to integrate new hires seamlessly into the organization.

iii Mutually Reinforcing:

HPHRPs mutually support and reinforce one another, creating a combined impact that is more potent than individual contributions. When practices such as performance feedback and recognition are implemented together, they synergistically enhance employee motivation and commitment.

iv Synergistic Impact on Firm's Performance:

The combined effect of HPHRPs results in a synergistic impact on the overall performance of the organization. The strategic integration of these practices contributes to the development of a positive organizational culture, attracting and retaining top talent, fostering innovation, and ultimately leading to improved organizational outcomes.

2.4 Overview of Delery and Doty's Research and Contribution

In response to the evolving demands and dynamic interplay of various factors including technological advancements, change in organizational structure and increased awareness of the pivotal role of employees in achieving strategic objectives of organizations (Schuler et al., 2001), HRM has undergone significant transformations. Decades were invested by researchers to unravel the transition from traditional HR practices to the dynamic realm of HPHRPs. Initially it was believed that individual HR practices could handle the workforce well by making employees feel that their organisation care about them. But Later on it has been realized that practices must be used in combination, and effort was put to create a universal set of best practices that may result in superior organizational performance (Tzafrir, 2006).

Before delving deeper into the universalistic approach, it is crucial to acknowledge the research and contributions of Delery and Doty. Until the 1980s, the existence of HPHRPs was a subject of debate. In the 1990s, Dr. John E. Delery and D. Harold Doty conducted extensive studies on the prevailing perspectives regarding the combination of HR practices. They categorized these perspectives into three main groups: Universalistic, Contingency, and Configurational. Delery and Doty's work laid the groundwork for understanding the various approaches to HPHRPs and highlighted the importance of tailoring HR practices to fit organizational contexts. Their insights have significantly influenced the ongoing discourse on effective human resource management strategies. Let's discuss each perspective one by one (Delery & Doty, 1996):

2.4.1 Universalistic Perspective of HPHRPs: One-Size-Fits-All Approach

The Universalistic approach also referred to as the Universalistic model or theory, centers around the development of a singular, optimal set of HR practices that are deemed universally applicable to all organizations. This perspective firmly asserts that adopting this standardized set of practices is inherently linked to achieving superior organizational performance across various contexts.

The core premise of the Universalistic approach rests on the belief that certain HR practices, when universally implemented, possess inherent qualities that contribute to organizational success irrespective of the industry, size, or specific organizational characteristics. Proponents of this approach argue that a one-size-fits-all strategy can streamline operations, enhance employee engagement, and ultimately lead to superior overall performance for each organization.

By advocating for a universal set of HR practices, the Universalistic approach simplifies the complexities associated with tailoring strategies to diverse organizational environments. This streamlined perspective, if proven effective, could offer a practical and efficient framework for organizations seeking a standardized approach to human resource management.

Many scholars and researchers tried to propose such best set of practices such as:

Pfeffer proposed seven practices for successful organizations, including (Pfeffer, 1998):

i   Employment security.

ii   Selective hiring of new personnel.

iii   Self-managed teams and decentralization of decision-making as fundamental principles of organizational design.

iv   Relatively high compensation tied to organizational performance.

v   Comprehensive training programs.

vi   Diminished status differentials and barriers, encompassing dress code, language usage, office arrangements, and wage variances across levels.

vii   Widespread dissemination of financial and performance data throughout the organization.

Many scholars and professionals were skeptical about the idea that there's a guaranteed connection between how a company manages its human resources (HRM strategy) and how well it performs as an organization. They argue against the belief that there's a single set of HR practices that can be applied everywhere and produce the same positive results for every organization, no matter their differences in context and goals. In essence, they're saying that what works for one company might not work for another, and there's no universal formula for success in managing human resources (Syed & Jamal, 2012). In other words, critics argue that organizational diversity and contextual variations may impact the universal applicability of such practices, warranting a more nuanced understanding of the complex interplay between HR strategies and organizational outcomes.

2.4.2   Contingency Perspective of HPHRPs: Context Matters in Strategic HRM

Contrary to the idea that one set of best HR practices fits all, contingency scholars argue that HR strategies work best when tailored to suit a specific organization and its environment. Unlike the straightforward relationships in universalistic thinking, contingency arguments are more complex, suggesting that interactions play a crucial role. These scholars believe that how HR practices fit within an organization's unique context impacts their effectiveness. For instance, certain HR practices may align better with different strategic positions within a company, affecting its overall performance.

To put it other way the contingency approach, also called the best-fit approach, rejects the notion of a one-size-fits-all HRM system. Instead, it emphasizes that HR strategies should align closely with an organization's business strategy and industry-specific factors. This approach assumes that organizations that integrate their business and HR strategies effectively will outperform those that don't. The idea is that the best outcomes occur when there's a strong match, or "best fit," between an organization's strategy and its HR practices.

Let's consider a practical example to illustrate the difference between universalistic and contingency approaches:

Universalistic Approach Example: In a universalistic approach, a company might adopt a standard set of HR practices across all departments and positions, believing that these practices will universally lead to improved organizational performance. For instance, they might implement a standardized performance appraisal system, uniform training programs, and a fixed compensation structure for all employees, assuming that these practices will work well regardless of the company's context.

Contingency Approach Example: In contrast, a company using a contingency approach would consider how various factors within its organization and environment might influence the effectiveness of HR practices. For example:

- **Performance Appraisal System:**

    - In a highly dynamic and innovative industry where creativity and adaptability are key, a company might find that traditional annual performance reviews are too inflexible. Instead, they might adopt a continuous feedback system or peer evaluations to promote agility and innovation.

- Conversely, in a more stable industry where consistency and reliability are valued, annual performance reviews might work well to provide clear expectations and goals for employees.

- **Training Programs:**

  - A company operating in a technology-driven sector might find that investing in specialized technical training for its employees is essential to keep up with rapid advancements.

  - However, a company in a service-oriented industry might prioritize customer service training and interpersonal skills development to enhance client satisfaction and loyalty.

- **Compensation Structure:**

  - In a competitive market where attracting and retaining top talent is crucial, a company might offer performance-based pay and bonuses to incentivize high performance.

  - Alternatively, in an industry where labor costs are a significant concern and turnover rates are high, a company might focus on offering competitive base salaries and benefits to ensure employee retention.

In this example, the contingency approach recognizes that the effectiveness of HR practices depends on various contextual factors such as industry dynamics, organizational strategy, and workforce characteristics. Therefore, HR practices need to be tailored to fit the specific needs and circumstances of each organization.

However, critics argue that the contingency approach overlooks other organizational and environmental factors that might impact the adoption of HR practices. For example, implementing a long-term HR strategy can be challenging if employees tend to leave quickly. This shows that just focusing on strategy alone might not be enough to gain a competitive edge. Furthermore, trying to link organizational strategy (like innovation or cost leadership) to HR strategy (such as job design or performance-based pay) isn't always straightforward. Critics say the contingency approach oversimplifies the complexities of organizational realities and practices

2.4.3 Configurational Perspective of HPHRPs: HR Practices as Integrated Elements

In the last few decades, some new ideas evolved supporting the contingency approach and went further suggesting that numerous bundles can be formed based on specific needs, and when these practices work together, they significantly enhance a firm's performance (Martín-Alcázar et al., 2005) . Essentially, each practice within a bundle strengthens the others, leading to a collective impact greater than the sum of the practices operating independently (Tharenou et al., 2007).

In other words, the Configurational perspective emphasizes the synergistic impact of aligning HR practices in specific combinations to enhance firm performance. It suggests that when HR practices are strategically integrated and complement each other, they can have a greater positive effect on organizational outcomes than when implemented individually. This perspective acknowledges that there are numerous combinations of HR practices that can be formed, and the effectiveness of these combinations depends on how well they align with the organization's strategy, culture, and goals.

For example, a company may find that combining rigorous recruitment and selection processes with extensive training and development programs, alongside a performance management system that provides regular feedback and recognition, leads to improved employee performance and organizational success. Each of these HR practices reinforces the others, creating a cohesive system that drives high performance.

Given the wide range of possible combinations, the configurational perspective suggests that organizations should carefully assess their

unique circumstances and select HR practices that fit together
harmoniously to maximize their impact on firm performance.

3. Black Box of High Performance HR Practices

3.1 Decoding the Black Box of HPHRPs

High Performance HR Practices encompass a range of strategies and initiatives designed to enhance organizational effectiveness. Over time, it has also emerged that effectiveness increases because these practices impact multiple organisational outcomes, such as productivity, profitability, growth, survival, and other performance metrics. However, one question has always troubled the scholars that how does this process happen, that is, do these practices directly affect the performance outcome or do some mediating factors also play a role in it?

Numerous studies sequentially investigated this topic, with one of the most compelling arguments being what we now recognize as the AMO Theory. This theory posits that HPHRPs function by nurturing enhanced skills, igniting motivation, and expanding opportunities for employee contribution (Appelbaum, 2000). It acknowledges the interconnectedness of HR practices in influencing these three factors that drive employee performance. In other words when high-performance work practices are aligned, employee performance is expected to reach its peak as a result of enhanced skills, increased motivation, and expanded opportunities for employee contributions.

Yet, the journey does not end here. Recent research has shed light on numerous crucial intermediate outcomes that serve as pivotal markers of organizational sustainability. Among these, four emerge as beacons guiding organizations towards longevity and prosperity: Employee Commitment, Perceived Organizational Support (POS), Employee's Turnover Intention, and Job Satisfaction.

In this chapter, we embark on an exploration of these critical intermediate outcomes, delving into each factor individually to unveil its significance and impact on organizational sustainability. By decoding these pivotal elements, we aim to equip organizations with the insights needed to navigate the complex landscape of HPHRPs and emerge as champions of effectiveness and resilience.

3.2 Intermediate Outcome 1: Employee Commitment

Organizational commitment has permeated contemporary management discussion to such an extent that its nuances often evade clear understanding. This oversight can result in a failure to grasp the depth of employee dedication to the organization, thereby impeding the effectiveness of management strategies. Consider, for instance, the scenario of an organization experiencing high turnover rates despite competitive compensation packages. A deeper understanding of organizational commitment may reveal that employees lack emotional connection to the company's values or objectives, resulting in their eventual disengagement, indicating low commitment due to diminished emotional attachment.

However, employee decisions to leave or stay can be influenced by various factors beyond emotional attachment alone, prompting researchers to devise different classifications of organizational commitment. Here, I aim to elucidate the complexities of organizational commitment by explaining its meaning and discussing the three recognized types extensively debated in research: Affective Commitment, Continuance Commitment, and Normative Commitment.

3.2.1 What is Organizational Commitment?

Organizational commitment can be gauged by how willing an individual is to embrace the values and objectives of the organization, fulfill their job duties, and exhibit positive behaviors in the workplace." Let's understand this with the help of an example:

"Mukesh works as a customer service representative at a telecommunications company. He always arrives on time, greets his colleagues with a smile, and consistently goes above and beyond to assist customers with their inquiries. Additionally, Mukesh actively participates in company meetings and initiatives aimed at improving customer satisfaction. He demonstrates a strong commitment to the organization by fully embracing its values of excellent customer service and teamwork, fulfilling his job duties with dedication, and exhibiting positive behaviors in the workplace. Mukesh's actions showcase his high level of organizational commitment."

During the 1990s, Allen and Meyer introduced a structured perspective on organizational commitment, dividing it into three distinct elements: affective, continuance, and normative commitment (Meyer et al., 1990). Affective commitment pertains to the emotional connection an employee has with the organization's values, reflecting their affinity towards it. Continuance commitment gauges an employee's readiness to persist in their employment with the same organization. Normative commitment involves the sense of duty or obligation an employee harbors towards the organization. While these three components of organizational commitment are interrelated and can influence each other, understanding them separately allows managers to tailor strategies to enhance each aspect effectively. By segmenting and visualizing these types of commitments, organizations can develop targeted approaches to strengthen employee engagement, retention, and loyalty based on the specific needs and priorities of their workforce.

3.2.2 Types of Organizational Commitment

Now, let's delve into each type individually and explore them thoroughly through the perspectives of researchers and academics.

i   Affective commitment

Affective commitment relates to the emotional bond that employees develop with their organization. It reflects the extent to which individuals identify with the values, goals, and mission of the organization, and how much they genuinely enjoy being part of it. Employees with high affective commitment are more likely to be loyal and motivated, contributing positively to the organizational culture and climate. As emphasized by Abraham Maslow, the innate goodness of people highlights the importance of providing affection and security to foster reciprocal feelings and behaviors. This sentiment underscores the growing emphasis on securing employees' affection and commitment via human resource practices. In today's competitive landscape, HR professionals are increasingly tasked with attracting, nurturing, and retaining talent to sustain a competitive edge. This imperative arises amidst economic uncertainties, rapid globalization, and the emergence of the workforce of millennial generation who are known for their high level of comfort and proficiency with mobile technology. Consequently, practitioners and scholars alike are focusing more on strategies to enhance employee affective commitment, recognizing its pivotal role in organizational success amidst such dynamic and challenging environments. This involves creating a supportive and inclusive work environment where employees feel valued, respected, and motivated to contribute to the organization's success.

For example, a company may implement initiatives such as mentorship programs, where senior employees provide guidance and support to newer hires, fostering a sense of belonging and loyalty. Another strategy could involve recognizing and rewarding employees for their contributions and achievements, thereby reinforcing positive feelings towards the organization.

Scholars in the field of organizational psychology and management are also conducting research to understand the factors that influence affective commitment and how it impacts organizational outcomes. This research helps organizations gain insights into the drivers of employee engagement and loyalty, allowing them to tailor their practices and policies accordingly.

Overall, by focusing on enhancing employee affective commitment, organizations can create a more resilient and cohesive workforce that is better equipped to navigate the challenges of today's business environment and drive organizational success.

Elevated levels of affective commitment among employees not only influence their willingness to remain with the organization (continuance commitment), but also inspire them to advocate for the organization and actively recruit others to join its talent pool. When employees feel deeply connected to their organization's values and mission, they naturally become enthusiastic ambassadors, promoting its reputation and attracting potential talent. For instance, imagine a marketing executive who is deeply passionate about the company's innovative approach to sustainability. This employee not only performs their job diligently but also shares their enthusiasm with friends, former colleagues, and industry contacts. They may actively encourage talented individuals to consider opportunities within the organization, citing its commitment to environmental responsibility as a key selling point.

Conversely, an employee who remains with the organization primarily due to a lack of alternative options (continuance commitment) but lacks emotional attachment to the company (affective commitment) can have detrimental effects. Such an individual might express dissatisfaction with the organization in their social circles, criticizing its practices or culture. This negative sentiment can tarnish the organization's reputation and deter potential recruits from considering employment opportunities. In simple words, fostering affective commitment among employees not only promotes retention but also cultivates a network of brand advocates who actively contribute to the organization's success. Conversely, overlooking the emotional connection employees have with the organization can lead to disengagement and potentially damage its reputation.

Finally, it's crucial to highlight the significant importance that recruiting managers place on the concept of person-organization fit. This emphasis is rooted in the desire to foster a strong sense of affective commitment among employees. Affective commitment tends to be stronger when there is alignment between the values of the individual and those of the organization. In other words, when there is minimal disparity between an employee's personal values and the values upheld by the organization, their emotional attachment to the company is likely to be higher.

Elaborating further, consider a scenario where a candidate strongly believes in environmental sustainability and social responsibility. If they join an organization that shares these same values and actively integrates them into its mission and practices, they are more likely to feel a deep sense of connection and commitment to the organization. Their passion for these values aligns with the organization's culture, fostering a harmonious relationship that enhances their dedication and engagement.

Conversely, if there is a significant mismatch between an individual's values and those of the organization, it can lead to feelings of dissonance and dissatisfaction. For example, if an employee values work-life balance but joins a company with a culture that prioritizes long hours and intense workload, they may struggle to connect with the organization on an emotional level. This misalignment can hinder their sense of commitment and ultimately impact their job satisfaction and retention.

Therefore, by prioritizing person-organization fit during the recruitment process, organizations can increase the likelihood of cultivating a workforce that is not only highly skilled but also deeply invested in the company's mission and values. This alignment fosters a positive organizational culture where employees feel valued, engaged, and motivated to contribute to the organization's success.**Continuance commitment**

Continuance commitment stems from the perceived disadvantages associated with leaving the organization, such as financial investments and challenges in securing alternative employment. It suggests that an employee's commitment to the organization is influenced by the investments they have made or the potential losses they would incur if they were to leave.

To illustrate, imagine an employee who has spent several years working for a company that offers extensive training programs and opportunities for skill development. Over time, they have invested significant time and effort in acquiring new skills and expertise through these programs. Additionally, they have also built a network of professional contacts within the organization. For this employee, the thought of leaving the company would mean losing these investments, both in terms of the time spent on training and the connections made within the organization. As a result, they may feel compelled to remain with the company, even if they are not completely satisfied with their job or the organizational culture.

In contrast to affective commitment, which is driven by emotional attachment and alignment with organizational values, continuance commitment is often independent or inversely related to positive work-related factors. For example, an employee may continue working for an organization primarily because they feel trapped by the financial implications of leaving, rather than because they find the work fulfilling or meaningful.

To put it simply, continuance commitment is based on the perceived costs associated with leaving the organization, rather than a genuine desire to remain. While affective commitment fosters engagement and loyalty based on emotional connection, continuance commitment may result in employees staying with the organization out of necessity rather than choice.

iii Normative commitment

Normative commitment is marked by a sense of duty or obligation, such as feeling compelled to stay with the organization or to endorse a new initiative. This commitment arises from an internalized belief in the moral or ethical responsibilities associated with one's role within the organization. For instance, imagine a long-term employee who feels a strong sense of loyalty to their company due to the support and opportunities it has provided throughout their career. Despite receiving enticing job offers from competitors, they choose to remain with their current employer out of a sense of obligation to repay the organization for its investment in their professional growth.

Similarly, consider a scenario where a company introduces a sustainability initiative aimed at reducing its environmental impact. Employees who believe in the importance of environmental stewardship may feel a sense of duty to support this initiative, even if it requires changes to their work processes or routines. Their normative commitment compels them to align their actions with the organization's goals and values, contributing to the success of the initiative. In short, normative commitment entails a sense of moral or ethical duty towards the organization, motivating employees to act in ways that uphold its interests and values, even when faced with competing alternatives or challenges.

Normative commitment, when viewed through the lens of lifetime commitment, reflects a deep-seated sense of loyalty and obligation that extends over the course of an individual's career. In this context, normative commitment is not just about staying with the organization in the present moment but also about making a long-term commitment to its goals, values, and success. For example, consider an employee who views their relationship with the organization as a lifelong commitment. They may have started their career with the company and intend to remain with it until retirement. This commitment is driven by a strong sense of loyalty and duty, as well as a belief in the organization's mission and values.

Throughout their career, this employee actively contributes to the organization's growth and development, taking on new challenges, supporting change initiatives, and mentoring younger colleagues. Their normative commitment guides their decisions and actions, leading them to prioritize the organization's interests above their own.

Even during times of uncertainty or change, such as restructuring or leadership transitions, the employee remains steadfast in their commitment to the organization. They may weather challenges and setbacks with resilience, drawing upon their sense of duty and dedication to navigate through difficult times. Overall, normative commitment in terms of lifetime commitment encompasses a deep sense of allegiance and responsibility towards the organization, driving employees to make enduring contributions and investments in its success over the course of their career.

3.3 How HPHRPs impact the Organizational Commitment?

3.3.1 HPHRPs and Affective Commitment

- High-performance HR practices that emphasize employee engagement, recognition, and empowerment contribute to affective commitment by fostering a positive work environment where employees feel valued and connected to the organization's mission.

- Opportunities for growth and development provided by HR practices also strengthen affective commitment as employees feel invested in the organization's future and are more likely to develop a sense of loyalty and attachment.

- Clear communication and transparency in HR practices build trust and credibility, which are essential for fostering affective commitment. When employees feel informed and included in decision-making processes, they are more likely to develop a sense of belonging and commitment to the organization.

3.3.2 HPHRPs and Continuance Commitment

- High-performance HR practices that provide competitive compensation, benefits, and job security can strengthen continuance commitment by reducing employees' perceptions of the costs associated with leaving the organization.

- HR practices that support work-life balance and employee well-being contribute to continuance commitment by reducing turnover intentions and increasing job satisfaction, making employees less likely to consider leaving the organization.

- Opportunities for skill development and career advancement provided by HR practices can also increase continuance commitment by enhancing employees' marketability and reducing their perceived reliance on the organization for future career opportunities.

3.3.3 HPHRPs and Normative Commitment

- HR practices that promote fairness, equity, and ethical behavior contribute to normative commitment by creating a sense of obligation to reciprocate the organization's investment in its employees.

- Opportunities for advancement and career development provided by HR practices can strengthen normative commitment as employees feel a sense of loyalty to an organization that supports their professional growth and success.

- Recognition and reward systems implemented through HR practices reinforce normative commitment by acknowledging employees' contributions and encouraging a sense of loyalty and commitment to the organization.

3.4 Intermediate Outcome 2: Perceived Organizational Support (POS)

Perceived Organizational Support (POS) is a fundamental concept in organizational psychology, reflecting employees' beliefs regarding their organization's appreciation of their contributions and concern for their well-being. It encompasses various dimensions, including fair treatment, supportive supervision, opportunities for growth, recognition, work-life balance, job security, and organizational justice. These dimensions significantly influence employees' perceptions of support within the workplace.

HR practices play a crucial role in shaping POS by creating a supportive work environment and demonstrating organizational commitment. Fair and transparent HR policies, effective leadership development, training programs, recognition and rewards, performance management, work-life balance initiatives, and open communication channels all contribute to enhancing POS.

The importance of POS lies in its implications for both employees and organizations. Employees with higher POS tend to exhibit greater job satisfaction, commitment, and engagement, leading to improved well-being and retention. Moreover, organizations with higher levels of POS experience lower turnover rates and absenteeism, contributing to cost savings and organizational effectiveness.

Furthermore, a positive reputation for supporting employees can enhance an organization's ability to attract and retain top talent, strengthening its employer brand and competitive advantage. Recognizing the significance of POS and implementing effective HR practices to enhance it is essential for fostering a positive work environment, improving employee outcomes, and driving organizational success.

3.5 Intermediate Outcome 3: Employee's Turnover Intention

Employee turnover intentions, the inclination or desire of an employee to leave their current job or organization, are pivotal in gauging workforce stability and organizational health. These intentions reflect employees' evaluations of their current job, career prospects, work environment, and overall fit within the organization. High turnover intentions can signal underlying issues such as dissatisfaction, lack of engagement, or perceived better opportunities elsewhere.

For organizations, understanding and managing turnover intentions are essential due to several reasons. Firstly, high turnover rates can result in significant costs associated with recruitment, training, and productivity losses. Constant turnover disrupts workflow, diminishes team cohesion, and erodes institutional knowledge, thereby impacting organizational performance and productivity. Moreover, frequent turnover can create a negative ripple effect on employee morale and engagement, leading to decreased motivation and commitment among remaining staff members.

Additionally, turnover intentions can influence an organization's reputation and employer branding. A reputation for high turnover rates can deter top talent from considering job opportunities within the organization and can tarnish its image among customers, suppliers, and other stakeholders. Therefore, it's imperative for organizations to address turnover intentions proactively to mitigate these adverse effects and maintain a positive organizational culture.

High-Performance HR Practices (HPHRPs) can significantly impact turnover intentions by fostering a supportive work environment, enhancing job satisfaction, and promoting organizational commitment. HPHRPs such as fair compensation, opportunities for advancement, recognition programs, and supportive leadership can bolster employee satisfaction and engagement, thereby reducing turnover intentions. Additionally, initiatives that support work-life balance, such as flexible work arrangements and wellness programs, can address employee needs and reduce the likelihood of turnover.

Moreover, effective communication and transparency within the organization, facilitated by HPHRPs, can help manage turnover intentions by addressing employee concerns, providing clarity on organizational goals and changes, and fostering trust and loyalty. By investing in HPHRPs that prioritize employee well-being, development, and engagement, organizations can mitigate turnover intentions, retain top talent, and cultivate a positive workplace culture that drives organizational success in the long term.

3.6 Intermediate Outcome 4: Job Satisfaction

Job satisfaction, the overall sentiment an individual holds towards their job and work environment, is pivotal for both employees and organizations. It encompasses various facets such as fulfillment of work-related needs, enjoyment derived from tasks, relationships with colleagues and supervisors, compensation, and opportunities for growth. For employees, job satisfaction contributes significantly to their well-being, mental health, and quality of life. Satisfied employees tend to exhibit higher levels of motivation, engagement, and commitment to their work, leading to increased productivity, job performance, and longevity in their roles.

From an organizational standpoint, job satisfaction directly impacts employee retention, turnover rates, and overall performance. Satisfied employees are more likely to remain with the organization, reducing turnover costs and preserving institutional knowledge. They also contribute to positive employer branding and customer satisfaction, ultimately driving organizational success and competitiveness.

High-Performance HR Practices (HPHRPs) play a crucial role in influencing job satisfaction by addressing various factors that impact employees' experiences in the workplace. HPHRPs encompass a range of human resource management strategies and initiatives aimed at maximizing employee potential, engagement, and organizational effectiveness.

For instance, fair and transparent policies foster trust and confidence among employees, while opportunities for growth and development fulfill their aspirations for career advancement and personal growth. Effective recognition programs and supportive leadership practices acknowledge employees' contributions and create a positive work environment conducive to higher job satisfaction. Moreover, work-life balance initiatives, such as flexible work arrangements and wellness programs, help employees manage their personal and professional responsibilities, enhancing their overall satisfaction and well-being.

Organizations that invest in high-performance HR practices are more likely to cultivate a satisfied, engaged, and productive workforce, leading to improved organizational outcomes and long-term success.

4. Indian Health Sector

4.1 Introduction

India's healthcare sector is significant globally due to its vast population, which currently exceeds 1.3 billion people. With such a large population, India faces unique challenges in providing adequate healthcare services to all its citizens. Despite being one of the fastest-growing economies globally, India's healthcare system still lags behind those of many developed nations in terms of infrastructure, accessibility, and quality of care.

In terms of healthcare expenditure as a percentage of GDP, India's spending is relatively low compared to other countries. According to the World Bank, India's healthcare expenditure was approximately 3.6% of its GDP in 2019, significantly lower than the global average of around 10%. This low expenditure reflects the challenges India faces in providing adequate healthcare services to its vast population.

A robust healthcare sector is essential for the overall development and well-being of a nation. In India, a healthy population is crucial for driving economic growth, reducing poverty, and achieving social stability. Additionally, a well-functioning healthcare system is essential for addressing public health challenges, controlling the spread of diseases, and improving life expectancy rates.

Investments in healthcare can yield significant returns in terms of improved productivity, reduced healthcare costs in the long run, and enhanced human capital development. Moreover, a healthy workforce is better equipped to contribute to economic growth and development.

4.2 Three-Tiered Structure

The Indian healthcare system is divided into three tiers to ensure comprehensive healthcare delivery across different levels:

4.2.1 Primary Healthcare

Primary healthcare forms the foundation of the healthcare system and focuses on preventive and basic healthcare services. Primary healthcare services are typically provided through primary health centers (PHCs), sub-centers, and community health workers. These services include immunizations, maternal and child health services, family planning, treatment for common illnesses, and health education and promotion.

Primary Health Centers (PHCs):

- PHCs are typically the first point of contact between the community and the healthcare system.

- They are responsible for providing a range of basic healthcare services, including preventive, promotive, curative, and rehabilitative care.

- PHCs are established and maintained by state governments, often under national healthcare programs.

- They are usually staffed by a medical officer and a team of paramedical and support staff.

- PHCs also act as referral points for more specialized care at higher-level healthcare facilities like CHCs and hospitals.

Sub Centres (SCs):

- SCs serve as the most peripheral and grassroots level of healthcare delivery.

- They are typically located within villages or small communities, making them easily accessible to the local population.

- SCs focus on providing basic preventive and primary healthcare services, often with an emphasis on maternal and child health, family planning, immunization, and disease prevention.

- They are manned by auxiliary nurse midwives (ANMs) or female health workers, along with male health workers.

- SCs play a crucial role in health education, community outreach, and promoting healthy behaviors within the local community.

Here's a comparison of Primary Health Centers (PHCs) and Sub Centres (SCs) in tabular form:

Aspect	Primary Health Centers (PHCs)	Sub Centres (SCs)
Scope of Services	Comprehensive: preventive, promotive, curative, rehabilitative care	Basic: preventive, maternal and child health, family planning, immunization, disease prevention
Level of Care	Higher, capable of managing a wide range of health conditions and emergencies	Basic, primarily focused on first-line healthcare provision
Staffing	Medical officer, paramedical staff, support staff	Auxiliary Nurse Midwives (ANMs), female health workers, male health workers
Catchment Area	Larger, covering multiple villages or a defined geographical region	Smaller, typically serving a single village or community

Nature of primary healthcare services:

Primary healthcare focuses on preventive care, health promotion, and basic treatment for common illnesses. Here are some examples of primary healthcare services:

Routine Check-ups: Primary healthcare providers, such as general practitioners (GPs) or family physicians, offer regular check-ups for individuals of all ages to monitor their overall health, screen for common health conditions, and provide preventive care recommendations.

Treatment of Common Illnesses: Primary care clinics manage and treat common health issues such as colds, flu, minor injuries, infections, allergies, and skin conditions. They also provide vaccinations and medications for these conditions.

Chronic Disease Management: Primary care providers play a central role in managing chronic conditions like diabetes, hypertension, asthma, and arthritis. They monitor patients' health status, prescribe medications, offer lifestyle counseling, and coordinate specialist care when needed.

Health Education and Counseling: Primary healthcare professionals provide health education and counseling on topics such as nutrition, exercise, smoking cessation, mental health, family planning, and preventive measures against diseases.

Maternal and Child Health Services: Primary care clinics offer prenatal care for pregnant women, including prenatal check-ups, screenings, and education on healthy pregnancy habits. They also provide pediatric care, including well-child visits, immunizations, and developmental screenings for infants and children.

Family Planning Services: Primary healthcare centers offer family planning services, including contraception counseling, access to contraceptives, and reproductive health screenings.

Referral Services: Primary care providers serve as gatekeepers to the healthcare system and refer patients to secondary and tertiary healthcare facilities for specialized care, diagnostic tests, surgeries, and other advanced medical interventions when necessary.

4.2.2. Secondary Healthcare

Secondary healthcare constitutes the next level in the healthcare system, where patients who require specialized treatment beyond what primary healthcare can provide are referred. In India, this tier encompasses facilities such as district hospitals and community health centers at the block level. These establishments are equipped with resources and expertise to diagnose and manage more complex medical conditions, catering to the needs of patients referred from primary care facilities.

Nature of secondary healthcare services

Specialized Surgery: If a patient requires a surgical procedure beyond the scope of a primary care clinic, such as a complicated orthopedic surgery or a cardiac procedure, they would be referred to a district hospital where specialist surgeons and operating theaters are available.

Chronic Disease Management: Patients with chronic conditions like diabetes or hypertension may require regular monitoring and specialized care. They might be referred to a community health center at the block level where doctors with expertise in managing chronic diseases can provide comprehensive care.

Advanced Diagnostic Services: For complex diagnostic tests like MRI scans, CT scans, or specialized blood tests, patients may need to visit a secondary healthcare facility like a district hospital where such advanced diagnostic services are available.

Emergency Care: In cases of medical emergencies that require intensive care units (ICUs), trauma care, or immediate specialist intervention, patients would be directed to secondary healthcare facilities equipped to handle such situations effectively.

Maternity Services: Pregnant women requiring specialized care during pregnancy, childbirth, or postnatal care may be referred to district hospitals or community health centers that offer maternity services with obstetricians, neonatologists, and necessary facilities for safe deliveries.

4.2.3 Tertiary Healthcare

Tertiary healthcare encompasses specialized medical services, advanced diagnostic procedures, and treatment for complex and specialized conditions. Tertiary care hospitals, often located in urban areas, are equipped with state-of-the-art medical technology, advanced diagnostic imaging facilities, intensive care units (ICUs), and specialized medical teams. These hospitals offer services such as cardiac care, neurosurgery, organ transplants, cancer treatment, advanced surgeries, and critical care.

Overall, the three-tiered structure of the Indian healthcare system aims to provide comprehensive healthcare services ranging from preventive and primary care to specialized tertiary care.

Demonstration of India's Three-Tiered Healthcare System through an Example:

Here's a scenario involving Ramesh, who lives in a rural area, seeking healthcare at different levels:

Ramesh, a 45-year-old farmer residing in a rural village, has been experiencing persistent chest pain and shortness of breath for the past few days. Concerned about his health, he decides to visit the primary healthcare center located in his village.

Primary Healthcare Visit: Ramesh visits the primary healthcare center where he consults with the resident general practitioner, Dr. Patel. After listening to Ramesh's symptoms and conducting a physical examination, Dr. Patel suspects that Ramesh may be experiencing cardiac issues and decides to conduct some basic tests such as an electrocardiogram (ECG) and blood pressure measurement. The tests reveal abnormal results, indicating a potential cardiac problem.

Referral to Secondary Healthcare: Recognizing the need for specialized care beyond what the primary healthcare center can provide,

Dr. Patel refers Ramesh to the district hospital located in the nearby town. Dr. Patel provides Ramesh with a referral letter detailing his medical history, symptoms, and initial test results to present at the district hospital.

Secondary Healthcare Visit: Ramesh travels to the district hospital and presents the referral letter to the reception desk. He is then directed to the cardiology department where he meets Dr. Gupta, a cardiologist. Dr. Gupta reviews Ramesh's medical history, conducts further diagnostic tests such as a stress test and echocardiogram, and confirms a diagnosis of coronary artery disease.

Treatment at Tertiary Healthcare: Due to the severity of Ramesh's condition and the need for advanced interventions, Dr. Gupta recommends that Ramesh undergo coronary angioplasty, a procedure to open blocked arteries in the heart. Ramesh is admitted to the tertiary healthcare facility, a specialized cardiac center in the nearby city, where the procedure is performed successfully by a team of interventional cardiologists.

Recovery and Follow-up: Following the procedure, Ramesh receives post-operative care at the tertiary healthcare center for a few days to ensure his recovery is progressing well. Once stabilized, he is discharged with medications and instructions for cardiac rehabilitation. Ramesh is advised to follow up with Dr. Gupta at the district hospital for regular check-ups and monitoring of his cardiac health.

This scenario demonstrates how Ramesh's journey through the healthcare system progresses from primary to secondary to tertiary levels, with each level providing increasingly specialized care tailored to his medical needs.

4.3 Challenges faced by Indian Healthcare Sector

Addressing the existing challenges and ensuring equitable access to quality healthcare for all citizens remain critical priorities for the Indian government and healthcare stakeholders. Below are listed some of the pressing challenges:

i **Accessibility:** Despite efforts to improve healthcare infrastructure, accessibility remains a significant challenge, particularly in rural and remote areas. Many rural regions lack adequate healthcare facilities, trained medical professionals, and essential medical supplies. This results in long travel distances and poor access to healthcare services for millions of people.

ii **Affordability:** Healthcare expenses can be a significant financial burden for many Indians, especially those from low-income households. Out-of-pocket expenditures for healthcare often lead to financial distress and push families into poverty. High healthcare costs, coupled with low insurance coverage, contribute to the affordability challenge, particularly for essential services and treatments.

iii **Quality of Care:** While India has skilled healthcare professionals and advanced medical technologies in urban areas, there are concerns about the quality of care provided, especially in government-run hospitals and primary healthcare centers. Issues such as overcrowding, inadequate infrastructure, shortage of medical supplies, and inconsistent adherence to clinical guidelines can compromise the quality of healthcare delivery.

iv **High turnover rates** in the Indian healthcare sector can indeed pose significant challenges to its sustainability. Here's how:

a *Impact on Continuity of Care:* High turnover rates among healthcare professionals, including doctors, nurses, and support staff, can disrupt the continuity of care for patients. When healthcare workers leave their positions frequently, patients may experience gaps in treatment, changes in care providers, and delays in accessing medical services. This can negatively affect patient outcomes and satisfaction levels.

b   *Quality of Care:* Continuity of care is crucial for ensuring the quality and effectiveness of healthcare services. Frequent turnover can lead to inconsistencies in care delivery, variations in clinical practices, and lapses in patient monitoring and follow-up. Healthcare organizations may struggle to maintain standards of care and implement quality improvement initiatives when faced with a revolving door of staff.

c   *Financial Impact:* High turnover rates can have financial implications for healthcare organizations, including recruitment and training costs, productivity losses, and decreased revenue due to vacancies and disruptions in service delivery. Constantly recruiting and training new staff members can strain limited financial resources and divert funds away from other critical areas of healthcare provision.

d   *Staff Morale and Job Satisfaction:* A high turnover environment can negatively impact staff morale and job satisfaction among healthcare professionals. Constant turnover can create a sense of instability, stress, and dissatisfaction among remaining staff members, leading to decreased motivation, engagement, and productivity. This can further exacerbate retention issues and perpetuate a cycle of turnover.

e   *Shortage of Skilled Professionals:* High turnover rates contribute to a shortage of skilled healthcare professionals in the industry. As experienced staff members leave their positions, healthcare organizations may struggle to attract and retain qualified replacements. This can lead to understaffing, increased workloads, and burnout among remaining staff, further compounding turnover issues.

f   *Negative Public Perception:* Persistent turnover within healthcare organizations can erode public trust and confidence in the healthcare system. Patients may perceive frequent staff turnover as a sign of instability, incompetence, or poor management, leading to dissatisfaction with healthcare services and a loss of faith in the healthcare system as a whole.

Addressing the problem of high turnover in the Indian healthcare sector requires a multifaceted approach that focuses on improving working conditions, enhancing job satisfaction, investing in professional development and training, implementing retention strategies, and addressing underlying systemic issues contributing to turnover. By prioritizing staff well-being and stability, healthcare organizations can improve sustainability, continuity of care, and overall quality of healthcare delivery.

4.4 Types of hospitals in India

In India, hospitals can vary widely in terms of size, services offered, ownership, and target patient population. Here are some common types of hospitals found in India:

i   Government Hospitals: These hospitals are owned and operated by the government at various levels, including central, state, and local government authorities. Government hospitals provide healthcare services to a large segment of the population, including primary, secondary, and tertiary care. They often offer services at subsidized rates or free of charge to low-income individuals.

ii   Private Hospitals: Private hospitals are owned and operated by private organizations or individuals. They vary in size and specialization, ranging from small nursing homes to large multi-specialty hospitals. Private hospitals typically offer a wide range of services, including primary care, specialized medical care, diagnostic services, and surgical procedures. Many private hospitals in urban areas are equipped with modern medical technology and provide high-quality healthcare services, albeit at higher costs compared to government hospitals.

iii Multi-Specialty Hospitals: Multi-specialty hospitals provide a comprehensive range of medical services across various specialties and subspecialties. These hospitals have departments dedicated to different medical specialties, such as cardiology, orthopedics, oncology, neurology, gynecology, and pediatrics. They offer advanced diagnostic and treatment facilities, including specialized equipment and medical expertise, to address a wide range of healthcare needs.

iv Super Specialty Hospitals: Super specialty hospitals focus on providing highly specialized medical care and treatment for complex and rare medical conditions. These hospitals are equipped with advanced medical technology and specialized medical professionals, including surgeons, physicians, and other healthcare specialists, with expertise in specific areas such as organ transplantation, cardiac surgery, neurosurgery, oncology, and pediatric surgery.

v Corporate Hospitals: Corporate hospitals are part of large corporate healthcare chains or hospital groups. These hospitals are often well-funded and professionally managed, with a focus on delivering high-quality healthcare services and achieving operational efficiency. Corporate hospitals may operate multiple facilities across different cities and regions, offering a wide range of medical services and amenities to patients.

vi Charitable Hospitals: Charitable hospitals are non-profit healthcare institutions that provide healthcare services to underserved communities and economically disadvantaged individuals. These hospitals often rely on donations, grants, and government subsidies to fund their operations and offer healthcare services at subsidized rates or free of charge to low-income patients. Charitable hospitals play a crucial role in expanding access to healthcare services for vulnerable populations.

vii Specialty Hospitals: Specialty hospitals focus on providing specialized medical care and treatment within a specific medical specialty or subspecialty. Examples include maternity hospitals (focused on obstetrics and gynecology), eye hospitals (focused on ophthalmology and eye care), orthopedic hospitals (focused on orthopedic surgery and musculoskeletal care), and cancer hospitals (focused on oncology and cancer treatment).

viii Teaching Hospitals: Teaching hospitals are affiliated with medical colleges and universities and serve as training sites for medical students, residents, and other healthcare professionals. These hospitals provide a combination of patient care, medical education, and research activities. Teaching hospitals often have academic departments, research centers, and facilities for medical training and education.

These are some of the common types of hospitals found in India, each catering to specific healthcare needs and serving different segments of the population.

4.5. The Diversity of Medicine Systems in India

India, with its rich history and diverse cultural heritage, is home to a multitude of medicine systems that have evolved over centuries. These medicine systems reflect the country's pluralistic approach to healthcare, where various traditional and modern practices coexist harmoniously. From ancient Ayurveda to modern allopathy, each medicine system in India offers unique insights into the art and science of healing.

Ayurveda, the ancient Indian system of medicine, is perhaps the most renowned and revered among all medicine systems in India. Originating over 5,000 years ago, Ayurveda is based on the principles of holistic healing, emphasizing the balance of mind, body, and spirit to achieve optimal health. Ayurvedic treatments encompass herbal remedies, dietary modifications, yoga, meditation, and lifestyle adjustments, making it a comprehensive system of healthcare.

Allopathy, also known as modern medicine, is widely practiced in India and is based on scientific principles and evidence-based practices. Allopathic treatments primarily involve the use of pharmaceutical drugs, surgery, and advanced medical technologies to diagnose and treat diseases. With its emphasis on empirical evidence and rigorous testing, allopathy has made significant advancements in medical research and healthcare delivery.

Homeopathy, another prominent medicine system in India, is based on the principle of "like cures like," where highly diluted substances derived from plants, minerals, and other natural sources are used to stimulate the body's self-healing abilities. Homeopathic remedies are selected based on individualized symptoms and constitutional factors, making it a personalized and holistic approach to healthcare.

Unani medicine, with its roots in ancient Greek and Persian traditions, is practiced widely in India, particularly in the northern regions. Unani medicine employs a holistic approach to healthcare, incorporating elements of Greek, Persian, and Ayurvedic medicine. Unani treatments often include herbal remedies, dietary advice, and lifestyle modifications to restore balance and harmony in the body.

Siddha medicine, originating in South India and attributed to Siddhar saints, is based on the concept of balancing the body's humors (doshas) to maintain health and treat diseases. Siddha remedies encompass herbal medicines, dietary modifications, yoga, and meditation, reflecting a holistic approach to healthcare deeply rooted in ancient wisdom.

Naturopathy, a system of alternative medicine, emphasizes natural healing modalities and the body's innate ability to heal itself. Naturopathic treatments may include dietary changes, herbal medicine, hydrotherapy, massage, acupuncture, and lifestyle counseling, promoting overall well-being and vitality.

The diversity of medicine systems in India is a testament to the country's cultural heritage, scientific advancements, and commitment to providing accessible and comprehensive healthcare to its citizens. While each system has its unique principles and practices, they all share a common goal: to alleviate suffering, restore health, and promote wellness in individuals and communities.

5. Exploring the Intricacies: Hospitals and the Challenge of Sustainable Workforce Management

Opening Vignette

As the sun rises over Mumbai, the hospital administration gears up for another day of managing the complex machinery that keeps the institution running. Among them is Mr. Patel, a seasoned administrator who understands the intricate nature of hospitals all too well.

From his office window, Mr. Patel observes the constant ebb and flow of patients, doctors, and nurses. He knows that hospitals are not just buildings—they are lifelines for communities, offering vital healthcare services that can make or break a nation's well-being.

Yet, as he reviews the latest turnover statistics, Mr. Patel can't help but feel a pang of concern. High employee turnover rates continue to plague the hospital, posing significant challenges to its operations. Every resignation means lost expertise, disrupted care, and increased strain on resources.

But the impact goes beyond the hospital walls. Mr. Patel understands that a sustainable health workforce is not just essential for the hospital's success—it's critical for the entire country. When hospitals struggle to retain staff, it affects the quality of care available to millions of people across India. It strains the healthcare system, undermines public trust, and threatens the nation's overall health and prosperity.

5.1 Need for Sustainable Health Workforce in India

The stability and sustainability of the healthcare workforce are paramount for the effective functioning of any healthcare system, and India is no exception. A robust and resilient workforce ensures that essential healthcare services are consistently available to meet the needs of the population. Let's delve deeper into why a sustainable health workforce is imperative for India:

i   **Meeting Healthcare Demands**: India has a large and diverse population with varying healthcare needs. A sustainable healthcare workforce ensures an adequate number of skilled professionals to meet the growing demand for healthcare services across urban and rural areas.

ii   **Addressing Health Disparities**: India faces significant health disparities between different regions, socio-economic groups, and urban-rural populations. A sustainable healthcare workforce can help bridge these gaps by providing equitable access to healthcare services and improving health outcomes for marginalized communities.

iii   **Managing Disease Burden**: India grapples with a high burden of communicable and non-communicable diseases, including infectious diseases, maternal and child health issues, and lifestyle-related conditions like diabetes and cardiovascular diseases. A sustainable healthcare workforce is essential for effectively preventing, diagnosing, and treating these health conditions.

iv   **Supporting Public Health Initiatives**: The Indian government implements various public health initiatives aimed at disease prevention, health promotion, and improving sanitation and hygiene. A sustainable healthcare workforce plays a crucial role in implementing these initiatives, conducting health education programs, and delivering preventive services to communities.

v   **Responding to Emergencies and Outbreaks**: India is vulnerable to natural disasters, disease outbreaks, and public health emergencies. A sustainable healthcare workforce with adequate training and preparedness is essential for effectively responding to such emergencies, providing timely medical care, and minimizing the impact on public health.

vi   **Driving Healthcare Innovation**: A sustainable healthcare workforce fosters a culture of innovation and continuous improvement in healthcare delivery. Skilled professionals contribute to research, technology adoption, and the development of new treatments and interventions, driving progress and advancements in the healthcare sector.

vii   **Economic Development**: A healthy population is essential for economic growth and development. A sustainable healthcare workforce contributes to productivity gains, reduces absenteeism due to illness, and minimizes healthcare costs associated with preventable diseases, ultimately promoting socio-economic development in India.

5.2   Current State of the Healthcare Workforce in India

India's healthcare workforce is vast and diverse, comprising various categories of healthcare professionals, including doctors, nurses, allied health professionals, and community health workers. However, despite its size, the healthcare workforce in India faces numerous challenges:

i   **Shortage of Skilled Professionals:** India continues to grapple with a shortage of skilled healthcare professionals, particularly in rural and remote areas. The uneven distribution of healthcare workers exacerbates disparities in access to healthcare services, with rural and underserved populations bearing the brunt of the shortage.

ii **Quality and Training:** While the quantity of healthcare professionals in India is significant, concerns regarding the quality of training and education persist. Variations in the quality of medical education and training programs contribute to disparities in clinical competencies and standards of care across different regions.

iii **Burnout and Attrition:** Healthcare professionals in India often face high levels of burnout and job dissatisfaction due to heavy workloads, inadequate resources, and challenging working conditions. Consequently, attrition rates are elevated, leading to frequent turnover and disruptions in healthcare delivery.

iv **Gender Disparities:** Gender imbalances persist within the healthcare workforce, with women often underrepresented in leadership positions and certain medical specialties. Addressing gender disparities is crucial for promoting diversity and ensuring equitable opportunities for healthcare professionals.

5.3 Factors Contributing to the Need for Sustainability

Several factors contribute to the imperative for sustainability within India's healthcare workforce:

i **Population Growth:** India's rapidly growing population places increased demands on the healthcare system, necessitating a corresponding expansion of the healthcare workforce to meet growing healthcare needs.

ii **Epidemiological Transition:** India is undergoing an epidemiological transition, with a shifting disease burden characterized by a rise in non-communicable diseases (NCDs) alongside persistent infectious diseases and maternal and child health challenges. Addressing this evolving disease profile requires a skilled and adaptable healthcare workforce capable of providing comprehensive care across various specialties.

iii **Healthcare Infrastructure Development:** The expansion of healthcare infrastructure, including the establishment of new hospitals, clinics, and healthcare facilities, requires a commensurate expansion of the healthcare workforce to staff these facilities adequately.

iv **Policy Reforms:** Evolving healthcare policies and reforms aimed at improving healthcare access, quality, and equity necessitate a responsive and adaptable healthcare workforce capable of implementing policy directives and meeting evolving healthcare standards.

In conclusion, the need for a sustainable health workforce in India is undeniable. Addressing the challenges facing the healthcare workforce and implementing measures to promote sustainability are critical steps toward ensuring that India's healthcare system remains resilient, responsive, and capable of meeting the healthcare needs of its diverse population.

5.4   Why hospitals are known for their intricate nature?

So far, we've understood the importance of sustainability in the Indian healthcare workforce and how it is affected by employee turnover. But did you know that nearly 60 percent of the Indian healthcare system is comprised of hospitals? Moreover, these hospitals have a very intricate nature. This complexity is viewed differently by organizations and employees. Without beating around the bush, let me directly state that such complexity plays a significant role in exacerbating employee turnover. Let's delve into both perspectives in detail.

Organizational Perspective:

a **Multifaceted Services**: Hospitals provide a wide range of medical services, including emergency care, surgery, diagnostic imaging, laboratory testing, pharmacy services, rehabilitation, and specialized treatments for various medical conditions.

Managing such diverse services requires intricate coordination and integration of resources, personnel, and facilities.

b **Complex Patient Needs**: Patients admitted to hospitals often have complex and acute medical conditions that require specialized care and treatment. Hospital staff must assess, diagnose, and manage patients' conditions effectively, often in high-pressure and time-sensitive situations.

c **Advanced Medical Technology**: Hospitals are equipped with advanced medical technology and equipment, including diagnostic imaging machines, surgical instruments, life support systems, and electronic health records systems. Managing and maintaining these sophisticated technologies require specialized training and expertise.

d **Regulatory Compliance**: Hospitals must adhere to stringent regulatory standards and accreditation requirements to ensure patient safety, quality of care, and compliance with healthcare laws and regulations. Achieving and maintaining regulatory compliance involves meticulous documentation, quality assurance processes, and ongoing staff training.

e **Interdisciplinary Collaboration**: Hospital care often involves interdisciplinary collaboration among various healthcare professionals, including physicians, nurses, pharmacists, therapists, and technicians. Coordinating care across different specialties and disciplines requires effective communication, teamwork, and shared decision-making processes.

f **Patient Flow and Capacity Management**: Hospitals must efficiently manage patient flow, including admissions, transfers, and discharges, to optimize bed utilization, minimize wait times, and ensure timely access to care. Balancing patient demand with available resources and capacity requires strategic planning and coordination across departments.

g **Emergency Preparedness**: Hospitals must maintain readiness to respond to emergencies, disasters, and mass casualty events. Developing comprehensive emergency preparedness plans, conducting drills and exercises, and coordinating with external agencies are essential components of hospital emergency management.

h **Ethical and Legal Considerations**: Hospitals face complex ethical and legal dilemmas related to patient care, privacy, consent, end-of-life decisions, and medical ethics. Addressing these issues requires careful consideration of ethical principles, legal obligations, and patient rights.

Employee Perspective

a **Diverse Skillsets and Specializations:** Hospital employees, including physicians, nurses, technicians, and administrative staff, possess diverse skillsets and specializations. Coordinating and integrating these varied roles and responsibilities within the hospital setting require effective leadership, communication, and teamwork.

b **High Workload and Stress:** Hospital employees often face high workloads and stress levels due to the demanding nature of their roles, long hours, and exposure to emotionally challenging situations such as patient emergencies, trauma cases, and end-of-life care. Managing workload and stress while maintaining focus and performance can be challenging for hospital staff.

c **Shift Work and Irregular Hours:** Many hospital roles require employees to work irregular hours, including nights, weekends, and holidays, to ensure 24/7 coverage of patient care services. Managing shift work and adjusting to irregular schedules can disrupt work-life balance and impact employee well-being and job satisfaction.

d **Continuous Learning and Skill Development:** Healthcare is a rapidly evolving field with advances in medical technology, treatment modalities, and healthcare practices. Hospital employees must engage in continuous learning and skill development to stay abreast of the latest developments and maintain competency in their respective roles.

e **Interdisciplinary Collaboration and Communication:** Hospital employees frequently collaborate with colleagues from different disciplines and departments to provide comprehensive patient care. Effective interdisciplinary collaboration requires clear communication, mutual respect, and an understanding of each other's roles and responsibilities.

f **Emotional and Ethical Challenges:** Hospital employees often encounter emotionally challenging situations, such as caring for critically ill patients, delivering bad news to families, and navigating end-of-life care decisions. Managing the emotional impact of these experiences and maintaining professionalism while upholding ethical standards can be daunting for hospital staff.

g **Bureaucratic and Administrative Burdens:** Hospital employees may face bureaucratic and administrative burdens associated with documentation requirements, regulatory compliance, and administrative tasks. Balancing clinical responsibilities with administrative duties can add to the complexity of their roles and contribute to burnout and frustration.

h **Career Advancement and Professional Growth:** Hospital employees may navigate complex career paths and opportunities for advancement within the healthcare system. Pursuing career goals, obtaining advanced certifications, and seeking professional development opportunities require strategic planning and navigation of organizational structures and policies.

5.5 Challenges posed by High Employee Turnover in Indian Health Sector

High employee turnover in the healthcare sector poses significant challenges for organizations and can have detrimental effects on patient care, staff morale, and organizational performance. Continuously changing healthcare providers disrupts continuity of care, leading to gaps in treatment and compromising patient safety and satisfaction. Moreover, remaining staff members face increased workloads and burnout as they take on additional responsibilities to compensate for vacant positions. The costs associated with recruitment, onboarding, and training of new employees further strain organizational resources. Additionally, the loss of experienced staff results in the depletion of valuable institutional knowledge and expertise, negatively impacting the quality of care provided. High turnover also disrupts team dynamics, leading to decreased collaboration and communication breakdowns. Furthermore, it can damage the organization's reputation, making it challenging to attract both patients and skilled healthcare professionals. To mitigate these challenges, healthcare organizations must implement strategies to improve employee retention, enhance workplace culture, offer competitive compensation and benefits, provide opportunities for professional development, and address underlying causes of turnover such as workload issues and staffing shortages. By fostering a stable and sustainable workforce, healthcare organizations can improve patient outcomes and ensure the delivery of high-quality care.

6. High Performance HR Practices and Workforce Sustainability in Healthcare Organizations: An Empirical Study based in Indore

In the preceding chapters, the focus has been on elucidating key concepts such as strategic Human Resource Management (HRM) and High Performance HR Practices (HPHRPs), along with their operational mechanisms. Additionally, insights have been provided into the structure and functioning of the Indian healthcare system. Central to this exploration has been the discussion on how HPHRPs contribute to the development of a resilient workforce within organizations, thereby fostering sustainability.

HPHRPs have been demonstrated to enhance organizational performance, with lower employee turnover being a significant indicator. Several studies have substantiated how HPHRPs effectively contribute to building a resilient workforce and influence factors such as employee commitment, Perceived Organizational Support (POS), and intention to leave. Recent researches indicated that HPHRPs, by promoting employee well-being, work-life balance, and job satisfaction, foster a supportive work environment that strengthens employees' commitment to the organization. Moreover, initiatives such as wellness programs, professional development opportunities, and flexible work arrangements provided through HPHRPs enhance employees' perception of organizational support, leading to increased loyalty and engagement. Additionally, HPHRPs play a crucial role in mitigating turnover intentions by addressing factors contributing to employee dissatisfaction and burnout, thereby promoting retention and stability within the workforce. Overall, HPHRPs are instrumental in creating a positive organizational climate that fosters employee resilience, commitment, and retention, ultimately driving improved performance and sustainability for the organization.

The endeavor has been to substantiate these assertions with robust evidence. Consequently, a research initiative was undertaken to examine the impact of HPHRPs on employees' turnover intentions, with the aim of demonstrating their role in enhancing the sustainability of Indian healthcare organizations. However, it's pertinent to note that due to practical constraints, it was challenging to encompass every organization in the study. Therefore, a selective approach was adopted, focusing on a few representative organizations.

Moving forward, the subsequent chapters will delve deeper into the findings and conclusions derived from this research endeavor. Beginning with an in-depth exploration of the relevant literature, the chapters will progress to elucidate the methodology employed in conducting the study, followed by a detailed analysis of the collected data. Through this structured approach, a comprehensive understanding of the research findings and their implications for practice will be provided, thereby enriching our comprehension of the interplay between HPHRPs, workforce dynamics, and organizational sustainability.

7. Literature Review

Before proceeding with my research, I conducted an extensive literature review with the aim of determining whether there is any research gap that I can address through my study. I did this because if research has already been conducted on the topic, then it would be a waste of time and resources to duplicate efforts. Additionally, such redundant research would be considered meaningless. I conducted this literature review in three phases, which are outlined as follows:

Phase 1: Employee Turnover Rate in Healthcare Organizations

In this initial phase, the review delves into understanding the employee turnover rate specifically within the context of healthcare organizations. It likely explores existing studies, reports, and data regarding the frequency and patterns of turnover within this sector. This phase sets the foundational understanding of the turnover dynamics within healthcare, identifying potential factors contributing to turnover and its implications.

Phase 2: Relationship between HPHRPs and Employee Turnover

The second phase shifts the focus towards examining the relationship between High-Performance Human Resource Practices (HPHRPs) and employee turnover. HPHRPs encompass various strategies and practices implemented by organizations to optimize employee performance, satisfaction, and retention. This phase likely involves scrutinizing literature to understand how the adoption and implementation of HPHRPs influence employee turnover rates within organizational settings. It may explore studies that investigate specific bundle of HR practices, and their impact on reducing turnover.

Phase 3: Literature Review on the Existence of HPHRPs in Healthcare Organizations

In the final phase, the review focuses on synthesizing literature that specifically addresses the existence and prevalence of High-Performance Human Resource Practices within healthcare organizations. This involves examining empirical research, theoretical frameworks, and case studies that highlight the adoption, implementation, and effectiveness of HPHRPs in healthcare settings. The objective is to gain insights into the extent to which healthcare organizations integrate and utilize high-performance HR practices to manage their workforce and address challenges such as turnover.

Note: *I have provided glimpses of the literature review in this book. The complete literature review is extensive, for which I will soon publish the second installment of this book.*

7.1 Literature Review on Employee Turnover in Healthcare sector

Authors: (Omanwar & Agrawal, 2021)

- **Corroborating Finding:** The study emphasized that there is a notable issue of substantial employee turnover within the Indian healthcare sector. It specifically aimed to explore how servant leadership influences two critical aspects: organizational identification and turnover intention. Servant leadership is a leadership style that prioritizes serving others and enhancing their growth and development. The study likely investigated whether this leadership approach affects how employees identify with their organization and whether it influences their intention to leave.

Authors: (Grover et al., 2018)

- **Corroborating Finding:** This study uncovered a significant turnover rate among doctors within the Indian healthcare sector. It suggests that turnover is a prevalent issue not only among general staff but also among highly skilled professionals like doctors. Understanding the turnover dynamics among doctors is crucial as it may have substantial implications for the quality of healthcare delivery and patient outcomes.

Authors: (Anand & Fan, 2016)

- **Corroborating Finding:** The research noted that the Indian health sector grapples with challenges related to employee turnover. It faces both a shortage of personnel and struggles to fill vacant positions with competent staff. This finding underscores the multifaceted nature of turnover challenges in the Indian healthcare system, encompassing issues of recruitment, retention, and skill shortages.

Authors: (Collini et al., 2015)

- **Corroborating Finding:** The study highlighted a significant turnover trend within the personnel of a major healthcare organization in the USA, particularly among nurses. It delved into various factors contributing to this phenomenon, indicating that turnover is not limited to specific regions but is a prevalent issue even in well-established healthcare systems like that of the USA. This emphasizes the global nature of turnover challenges in healthcare and the importance of understanding its underlying causes for effective intervention strategies.

Authors: (Dasgupta, 2014)

- **Corroborating Finding:** High rates of employee turnover were identified specifically among private hospitals in Kolkata, India. This indicates that turnover is not only a generalized issue within the Indian healthcare sector but is particularly pronounced in the private hospital setting in Kolkata. Understanding the specific context of turnover within private hospitals can help in devising targeted retention strategies tailored to the needs of this segment of the healthcare workforce.

Authors: (Bhattacharya et al., 2012)

- **Corroborating Finding:** The study emphasized the attrition of the healthcare knowledge workforce, encompassing both rural and urban areas in the northern regions of India. This suggests that turnover is not confined to specific geographic locations or types of healthcare organizations but is widespread across diverse settings, including both public and private sectors. The inclusion of rural areas highlights the broader scope of turnover challenges, which can have significant implications for healthcare access and delivery in underserved regions.

Authors: (Hogan et al., 2007)

- **Corroborating Finding:** The study found a shortage of nursing staff, particularly in acute care settings within hospitals in Australia. This indicates that turnover is not solely an issue in developing countries but also affects healthcare systems in developed nations like Australia. The shortage of nursing staff in acute care settings underscores the critical importance of addressing turnover challenges to ensure adequate staffing levels and maintain the quality of patient care.

Authors: (Zurn et al., 2005)

- **Corroborating Finding:** The research identified a significant turnover rate among healthcare employees across multiple developing and developed countries, including the UK, USA, and various African nations. Additionally, it highlighted the variation in turnover rates among healthcare institutions within the same country. This emphasizes the global nature of turnover challenges in healthcare and underscores the need for comprehensive strategies to address turnover at both national and organizational levels.

7.2 Literature Review on HPHRPs and employee Turnover

Authors: (Siyal et al., 2020)

- **Corroborating Finding:** Siyal et al. highlighted that High-Performance Human Resource Practices (HPHRPs) play a crucial role in aligning employees' values and goals with those of the organization. This alignment reduces emotional exhaustion and the desire to leave the organization. Essentially, when employees feel that their values and goals are in sync with the organization's mission and objectives, they are more likely to remain committed and engaged.

Authors: (Qureshi, 2019)

- **Corroborating Finding:** Qureshi emphasized that HPHRPs facilitate the retention of skilled employees, even when they receive tempting offers from other firms. This suggests that organizations that implement HPHRPs effectively are better equipped to retain their top talent, despite external competition.

Authors: (Fahim, 2018)

- **Corroborating Finding:** Fahim suggested that HPHRPs serve as strategic tools for organizations, enhancing their capabilities by ensuring the availability and retention of skilled labor. This underscores the strategic importance of HPHRPs in talent management and organizational effectiveness.

Authors: (Semedo, 2017)

- **Corroborating Finding:** Semedo argued that implementing high-performance HR practices, including skill development and motivation initiatives, enhances job satisfaction and encourages employee retention. This suggests that HPHRPs contribute to creating a positive work environment that fosters employee loyalty.

Authors: (Pittino et al., 2016)

- **Corroborating Finding:** Pittino et al. suggested that HPHRPs contribute to enhancing employee retention by fostering social exchange relationships within the organization. This emphasizes the importance of interpersonal connections and supportive work environments in reducing turnover.

Authors: (Rani & Gandotra, 2015)

- **Corroborating Finding:** Scholars argued that HPHRPs help reduce employee turnover by mitigating employee exhaustion. This indicates that bundle of practices aimed at improving work-life balance and reducing stress can contribute to higher retention rates.

Authors: (Ghosh et al., 2013)

- **Corroborating Finding:** Ghosh et al. suggested that HPHRPs empower employees by providing autonomy, growth opportunities, flexibility, and encouragement to excel, which positively impacts their decision to stay with the organization. This highlights the importance of empowering employees and creating a supportive work environment in retaining talent.

Authors: (Haines III et al., 2010)

- **Corroborating Finding:** Haines et al. argued that HPHRPs enable organizations to offer more appealing employment options, thereby enhancing employee retention. This suggests that organizations that invest in HPHRPs are more attractive to employees seeking long-term career growth and development.

Authors: (Bhatnagar, 2007)

- **Corroborating Finding:** Bhatnagar suggests that a unified set of HR practices cultivates a positive organizational culture, provides career opportunities, and offers crucial support, thereby reducing employees' intentions to quit. This underscores the role of organizational culture and support systems in retaining talent.

Authors: (Hiltrop, 1999)

- **Corroborating Finding:** Hiltrop argued that an array of interrelated HR practices fosters comprehensive employee development, aiding in employee retention. This suggests that a holistic approach to HR management, encompassing various practices, is essential for retaining talent.

Authors: (Huselid, 1995)

- **Corroborating Finding:** Huselid suggested that a bundle of HR practices positively influences employees' perceptions of their jobs, thus reducing their inclination to resign. This underscores the importance of a comprehensive HR strategy in shaping employees' experiences and retention.

7.3 Literature Review on HPHRPs in Health Sectors

Authors: (Rubel et al., 2021)

- **Corroborating Finding:** Rubel et al. reported that High-Performance Human Resource Practices (HPHRPs) are being utilized in private hospitals in Bangladesh. This indicates the adoption of such practices in the healthcare sector of Bangladesh's private healthcare institutions.

Authors: (Nasiru & Kwabe, 2020)

- **Corroborating Finding:** Nasiru and Kwabe found the prevalence of HPHRPs in general hospitals in Nigeria. This suggests that HPHRPs are not limited to specific types of healthcare institutions but are also present in general hospitals across Nigeria.

Authors: (Mohd Nasurdin et al., 2020)

- **Corroborating Finding:** Mohd Nasurdin et al. reported the existence of HPHRPs in Malaysian private hospitals. This indicates the adoption of HPHRPs within the private healthcare sector of Malaysia.

Authors: (Kloutsiniotis & Mihail, 2019)

- **Corroborating Finding:** Kloutsiniotis and Mihail identified HPHRPs in hospitals located in Athens and Thessaloniki, Greece. Additionally, they studied the impact of these practices on job satisfaction and the affective commitment of staff. This suggests that HPHRPs are present in Greek hospitals, and their effects on employee outcomes are being studied.

Authors: (Mahmoud & El-Sayed, 2016)

- **Corroborating Finding:** Mahmoud and El-Sayed marked the presence of HPHRPs in the Egyptian health sector and studied their impact on the quality of patient care. This indicates the adoption of HPHRPs within the healthcare sector of Egypt and their potential influence on patient care outcomes.

Authors: (Fan et al., 2014)

- **Corroborating Finding:** Fan et al. found HPHRPs in Chinese healthcare organizations. This suggests that HPHRPs are implemented within the healthcare sector of China.

Authors: (Leggat et al., 2011)

- **Corroborating Finding:** Leggat et al. found HPHRPs in Australian healthcare organizations. This indicates the presence of HPHRPs within the healthcare sector of Australia.

Authors: (Bonias et al., 2010)

- **Corroborating Finding:** Bonias et al. showed the presence of HPHRPs in Australian hospitals. This corroborates the finding from Leggat et al. and further confirms the adoption of HPHRPs in Australian healthcare institutions.

Authors: (Boselie, 2010)

- **Corroborating Finding:** Boselie demonstrated the implementation of high-performance work practices (HPWPs) within the Dutch healthcare sector. This emphasizes the adoption of similar practices in the healthcare sector of the Netherlands, focusing on improving individual employee ability, motivation, and opportunities.

Authors: (Scotti et al., 2007)

- **Corroborating Finding:** Scotti et al. highlighted the presence of HPHRPs in the Veteran healthcare sector. This indicates that HPHRPs are implemented within healthcare institutions serving veterans, emphasizing the importance of such practices in specialized healthcare settings.

7.4 Research Gap based on Literature Review

The literature review highlights a significant challenge in the health sector—employee shortage resulting from a notable turnover rate, among both clinical and non-clinical staff. This issue is particularly severe in India due to its large population and a growing burden of diseases. While literature acknowledges the use of High-Performance Human Resource Practices (HPHRPs) for building a resilient and sustainable workforce in healthcare institutions globally, there is a gap in research specifically addressing private hospitals in Indore, Madhya Pradesh. Therefore, the current study aims to fill this gap by focusing on the HPHRPs and their impact on employee's turnover intentions in this specific context.

8. Research Methodology

8.1   Rationale

The healthcare sector faces persistent challenges globally, with employee turnover disrupting organizational sustainability and patient care continuity. High-Performance Human Resource Practices (HPHRPs) have been recognized as effective strategies for mitigating turnover and fostering a resilient workforce in healthcare institutions. However, there exists a notable research gap concerning the utilization and impact of HPHRPs within the context of private hospitals in Indore, Madhya Pradesh.

Indore, situated in the heart of Madhya Pradesh, presents a unique healthcare landscape characterized by diverse providers and patient populations. Despite the significance of private hospitals in the region's healthcare delivery, empirical research focusing on HPHRPs within this sector is lacking.

Understanding the effectiveness of HPHRPs in private hospitals in Indore is crucial for maintaining healthcare quality and patient satisfaction. Therefore, this study aims to address this gap by identifying the HPHRPs implemented in these hospitals, assessing their effectiveness in mitigating turnover, and exploring factors influencing employees' turnover intentions.

In other words, by focusing on this specific context, the study seeks to advance knowledge and contribute to building a resilient and sustainable healthcare workforce to meet the region's evolving healthcare needs.

8.2   Objectives

i   To explore the adoption of HPHRPs within the healthcare organisations.

ii   To study the impact of HPHRPs on employee's turnover intentions in the healthcare organisations.

8.3   Research Methodology

8.3.1   Nature of the Study

The research is both exploratory and descriptive in its approach.

Exploratory Approach:

The exploratory aspect of the research denotes that the study seeks to investigate relatively uncharted territory within its field. In this case, the focus is on examining the utilization and impact of High-Performance Human Resource Practices (HPHRPs) within private hospitals in Indore, Madhya Pradesh. Given the limited existing research specifically addressing this topic in the context of the study area, an exploratory approach is appropriate. This approach allows the researcher to gather preliminary insights, identify patterns, and generate hypotheses for further investigation. Through exploratory research, the study aims to uncover new perspectives, challenges, and opportunities related to HPHRPs in the healthcare sector of Indore.

Descriptive Approach:

On the other hand, the descriptive aspect of the research refers to its intention to provide a comprehensive overview and description of the phenomena under investigation. In this case, the focus is on providing a detailed account of the utilization and impact of HPHRPs within private hospitals in Indore. This involves describing the specific HPHRPs implemented by these hospitals, assessing their prevalence, and examining their effectiveness in mitigating turnover and enhancing workforce stability. Through a descriptive approach, the study aims to paint a clear picture of the current state of HR practices within private hospitals in Indore, shedding light on key practices, challenges, and outcomes.

Combining exploratory and descriptive approaches allows the study to achieve multiple objectives. The exploratory aspect enables the researcher to uncover new insights and generate hypotheses, while the descriptive aspect provides a detailed and systematic account of the phenomena under investigation. Together, these approaches facilitate a comprehensive understanding of the utilization and impact of HPHRPs within private hospitals in Indore, laying the groundwork for future research and informing practical interventions to address workforce-related challenges in the healthcare sector.

8.3.2 Population

Staff members working in private hospitals located Indore.

This population consists of individuals across different job roles and departments within private hospitals, including but not limited to:

Healthcare Professionals: This category includes doctors, nurses, pharmacists, laboratory technicians, radiologists, and other clinical staff directly involved in patient diagnosis, treatment, and care delivery.

Administrative Staff: Administrative staff members play a crucial role in managing hospital operations, handling patient admissions, scheduling appointments, managing medical records, and coordinating with other departments.

8.3.3 Sample Size

The study aims to include a total of 370 employees working in private hospitals located in Indore, Madhya Pradesh. The sample encompasses both clinical and non-clinical staff members to ensure a comprehensive representation of the healthcare workforce within these hospitals.

The selection of a sample size of 370 employees for the study is guided by the statistical constraints of the central limit theorem. The central limit theorem is a fundamental concept in statistics that states that as the sample size increases, the distribution of sample means approaches a normal distribution, regardless of the shape of the population distribution.

Rationale for Sample Size:

Statistical Reliability: By drawing a sample size of 370 employees, the study aims to ensure statistical reliability and precision in the estimation of population parameters. A larger sample size provides greater confidence in the representativeness of the sample and the accuracy of the findings.

Normal Distribution Assumption: The central limit theorem suggests that with a sufficiently large sample size, the distribution of sample means will approximate a normal distribution, regardless of the underlying distribution of the population. This assumption allows for the application of parametric statistical tests, which rely on the normality of sample distributions for accurate inference.

Margin of Error: The chosen sample size of 370 employees allows for a manageable margin of error in estimating population parameters. A smaller margin of error increases the precision of the estimates, providing more reliable insights into the utilization and impact of High-Performance Human Resource Practices (HPHRPs) within the population of private hospitals in Indore.

Selection Criteria for Respondents:

Minimum Salary Requirement: Each respondent must have a monthly salary of at least 15,000 or more.

Selection Criteria for Hospitals:

The selection of private hospitals for inclusion in the study is based on specific criteria to ensure a diverse and representative sample. The selected hospitals must meet the following criteria:

Minimum Bed Capacity: Each selected hospital must have a minimum bed capacity of 100 beds. This criterion ensures that the included hospitals are of sufficient size and scale to accommodate a substantial workforce, reflecting the diversity of healthcare services and operations.

Hospital Names: The study identifies 14 private hospitals in Indore that meet the minimum bed capacity requirement. These hospitals are as follows:

i   Medanta Hospital

ii   Bombay Hospital

iii Choithram Hospital

iv SAIMS Hospital

v   Shalby Hospital

vi Rajshree Apollo Hospital

vii Life Care Hospital

viii Gokuldas Hospital

ix Vishesh Jupiter Hospital

x   Suyash Hospital

xi Arihant Hospital

xii Greater Kailash Hospital

xiii CHL Hospital

xiv Bhandari Hospital

8.3.4   Sampling Technique

Convenience sampling (Participants were selected based on their availability and accessibility.)

8.3.5   Data Collection Tool

Questionnaire Structure:

The primary data collection employed a standardized questionnaire comprising three distinct sections:

Part 1: Demographic Information

Part 2: High-Performance Human Resource Practices (HPHRPs)

Part 3: Employees' Turnover Intentions

Scale Utilization:

- The HPHRPs section utilized a 29-item scale developed by (Danayiyen & Bekaroglu, 2020).

- To measure employees' turnover intentions, the TIS-6 scale developed by (Bothma & Roodt, 2013) was employed.

Validity and Reliability Reassessment:

Given the scales' age and the significant variations within the target population (e.g., geographical distribution, age groups), a reassessment of their validity and reliability was undertaken (Awal, 2022).

Content Validity: Content validity was ensured by administering the questionnaire to 12 experts. Lawshe's content validity ratio was calculated, leading to the exclusion of 2 items with a CVR value below 0.56.

Reliability Assessment: A pilot survey involving 97 respondents was conducted to assess reliability. Reliability was determined using Cronbach's alpha coefficient.

8.3.6 Data Analysis Tool

Objective Wise Data Analysis Tool		
S.No.	**Objective**	**Tool**
1.	To explore the adoption of HPHRPs within the healthcare organisations	Exploratory Factor Analysis
2.	To study the impact of HPHRPs on employee's turnover intentions in the healthcare organisations.	Regression Analysis

8.3.7 Software Used

SPSS version 22.0

9. Data Analysis

Demographic analysis					
		Frequency	**Percent**	**Valid Percent**	**Cumulative Percent**
Job Type	Clinical	106	28.6	28.6	28.6
	Non-Clinical	264	71.4	71.4	100.0
Total		370	100.0	100.0	
Gender	Male	162	43.8	43.8	43.8
	Female	208	56.2	56.2	100.0
Total		370	100.0	100.0	
Age	Below 30 yrs	98	26.5	26.5	26.5
	30-40 yrs	126	34.1	34.1	60.5
	40-50 yrs	111	30.0	30.0	90.5
	Above 50	35	9.5	9.5	100.0
Total		370	100.0	100.0	

Reliability Statistics		
Construct	**Cronbach's Alpha**	**No. of Items**
HPHRPs	.935	27
Employee's Turnover Intention	.933	6
All Items	.825	33

The table above displays the outcomes of the Cronbach's alpha reliability test. Each value exceeded 0.6, indicating a high level of internal consistency.

Objective 1: Factor analysis was performed to achieve the first objective. The KMO test indicated good sample adequacy with a value above 0.5 (ranging from 0.70 to 0.80). Bartlett's test of sphericity was significant at 0.000 (P < 0.005). The summarized results are presented in the table 1.4.

KMO and Bartlett's Test		
Kaiser-Meyer-Olkin Measure of Sampling Adequacy.		.749
Bartlett's Test of Sphericity	Approx. Chi-Square	13036.844
	Df	351
	Sig.	.000

The initial solution revealed a total of five factors with Eigen values exceeding 1, collectively explaining 76.57% of the variation. The detail of which is shown below in table 1.5.

Total Variance Explained									
Component	Initial Eigenvalues			Extraction Sums of Squared Loadings			Rotation Sums of Squared Loadings		
	Total	% of Variance	Cumulative %	Total	% of Variance	Cumulative %	Total	% of Variance	Cumulative %
1	11.832	43.823	43.823	11.832	43.823	43.823	8.329	30.847	30.847
2	3.422	12.673	56.495	3.422	12.673	56.495	3.777	13.991	44.838
3	2.410	8.925	65.421	2.410	8.925	65.421	3.414	12.644	57.482
4	1.521	5.633	71.053	1.521	5.633	71.053	2.589	9.589	67.072
5	1.491	5.522	76.575	1.491	5.522	76.575	2.566	9.504	76.575

Extraction Method: Principal Component Analysis.

Rotated Component Matrix[a]					
	Component				
	1	2	3	4	5
Item 24	.861				

Item 25	.859				
Item 21	.854				
Item 27	.839				
Item 20	.834				
Item 23	.792				
Item 5	.768				
Item 26	.737				
Item 7	.643				
Item 10	.640				
Item 22	.605				
Item 8	.566				
Item 4	.548				
Item 15	.542				
Item 9	.532				
Item 14		.856			
Item 13		.805			
Item 12		.798			
Item 16		.642			
Item 17		.560			
Item 11			.763		

Item 3			.730		
Item 6			.685		
Item 1				.865	
Item 2				.536	
Item 18					.858
Item 19					.768
Extraction Method: Principal Component Analysis.					
Rotation Method: Varimax with Kaiser Normalization.					
a. Rotation converged in 14 iterations.					

Objective 2: To study the impact of HPHRPs on employee's turnover intentions in the healthcare organisations.

Hypothesis Testing

Ho 1: There is no significant relationship between HPHRPs and Employee's Turnover Intention.

Model Summary				
Model	R	R Square	Adjusted R Square	Std. Error of the Estimate
1	.687[a]	.472	.471	.93699
a. Predictors: (Constant), HPHRPs				

ANOVA[a]

Model		Sum of Squares	Df	Mean Square	F	Sig.
1	Regression	289.287	1	289.287	329.504	.000[b]
	Residual	323.085	368	.878		
	Total	612.372	369			

a. Dependent Variable: Employee's Turnover Intention

b. Predictors: (Constant), HPHRPs

Coefficients[a]

Model		Unstandardized Coefficients		Standardized Coefficients		
		B	Std. Error	Beta	T	Sig.
1	(Constant)	5.428	.187		28.963	.000
	HPHRP	-.961	.053	-.687	-18.152	.000

a. Dependent Variable: Employee's Turnover Intention

Interpretation: The outcomes of the regression analysis, as presented in Tables 7, 8, and 9, demonstrate the rejection of the null hypothesis Ho1. The results indicate that HPHRPs significantly predict Employee's Turnover Intention, as evidenced by $F(1, 368) = 329.504$, $p < 0.05$. This suggests a noteworthy role of HPHRPs in influencing Employee's Turnover Intention ($b = .687$, $p < 0.05$). The R^2 value of 0.472 indicates that HPHRPs account for 47.2% of the variance in Employee's Turnover Intention.

10. Discussion and Conclusion

10.1 Discussion

71.4% of the total respondents belonged to the non-clinical employee category. This indicates a substantial representation from individuals outside the clinical domain within the surveyed population. Moreover, the fact that 56.2% of the respondents were female indicates a significant representation of women in the study sample. This balanced gender representation enables a more nuanced examination of any potential gender-related disparities in the context of the study's objectives. Additionally, there was a predominant representation of respondents falling within the age range of 30 to 50 years. The dominance of respondents within this age bracket suggests a focus on a cohort that likely possesses considerable work experience and tenure.

The outcomes of the factor analysis unveiled five overarching categories of HR practices. Specifically, the first factor encompassed a total of 15 items, all associated with initiatives geared towards skill improvement, support for team development, training on legal aspect and related organizational endeavours. Consequently, the author assigned the label "training and development" to this factor. This practice underscores the organization's commitment to nurturing the professional growth and capabilities of its workforce. This strategic emphasis not only reflects a proactive approach to talent development but also communicates a commitment to staying abreast of industry trends and fostering a skilled, adaptable, and empowered workforce.

Likewise, the factor analysis identified five items under the second factor, three items under the third factor, two items under the fourth factor, and two items under the fifth factor. These factors were designated as Compensation, Employment Security, Performance Appraisal, and Post-Employment Security Practices, respectively. This delineation highlights the organization's deliberate focus on distinct aspects of its human resource management strategy. The "Compensation" factor indicates a targeted approach towards remuneration practices, reflecting the organization's commitment to fair and competitive pay structures. The "Employment security" factor suggests the organization's commitment to fostering a work environment that prioritizes the well-being and confidence of its employees in terms of job tenure. Similarly, the "Performance Appraisal" factor underscores the organization's commitment to assessing and enhancing employee performance systematically. Lastly, the "Post-Employment Security Practices" factor implies a thoughtful consideration of measures and policies addressing job security post-employment, showcasing the organization's concern for the well-being and stability of its workforce beyond their active service period.

The regression analysis findings revealed that 47.2% of the fluctuation in Employee's Turnover Intention can be attributed to Human Resource Practices (HPHRPs). This suggests a noteworthy impact of HPHRPs on the variability observed in employees' intentions to leave, highlighting the pivotal role of these practices in influencing turnover outcomes within the organization.

10.2 Conclusion

The comprehensive study conducted sheds light on critical challenges within Indian healthcare organizations. First and foremost, the literature review underscores the pressing issues of both a high employee turnover rate and a shortage of qualified staff in these organizations. This points to a significant human resource management challenge that requires attention. Building upon this, the study emphasizes the proactive adoption of HPHRPs, particularly noticeable in the private hospitals of Indore. This strategic focus on HPHRPs signifies recognition of the pivotal role played by human resource management in the healthcare sector, especially within a competitive landscape.

Zooming in on the organization's core priorities, the study underscores a multifaceted approach. The organization places a primary emphasis on crucial aspects such as training and development, compensation, employment and post-employment security, and performance appraisal. These practices are strategically employed to positively influence employee behavior, with a clear goal in mind: achieving the best possible patient outcomes.

The research findings reveal a noteworthy correlation between the application of HPHRPs in healthcare organisations and the reduction of employee turnover intentions. This emphasizes the pivotal role that HPHRPs play in fostering the development of a resilient and adaptable workforce, thereby contributing to the establishment of a sustainable organizational framework.

This study has important implications for academia, society, and the healthcare industry. For academics, it offers opportunities for further research and curriculum enhancement. In society, the adoption of HPHRPs can enhance patient care and contribute to job satisfaction and retention among healthcare professionals. In the healthcare industry, the findings suggest potential benefits in terms of operational efficiency, cost management, and strategic planning. Overall, the study provides a foundation for advancing sustainable human resource practices in healthcare settings. As the study is confined to 100-bedded private hospitals in Indore, it opens avenues for additional research on similar constructs within different healthcare organizations.

References

Appelbaum, E. (2000). *Manufacturing Advantage: Why High-performance Work Systems Pay Off.* Cornell University Press.

Awal, Dr. (2022). *Re: When do you validate an existing scale?* https://www.researchgate.net/post/When_do_you_validate_an_existing_s cale/63a74af12fef6b430e0cc769/citation/download

B.Becker. (1998). High performance work systems and firm performance: A synthesis of research and managerial implications. *Research in Personnel and Human Resources Management, 16,* 53.

Bhatnagar, J. (2007). Talent management strategy of employee engagement in Indian ITES employees: Key to retention. *Employee Relations, 29*(6), 640–663.

Bhattacharya, I., Ramachandran, A., Suri, R., & Gupta, S. (2012). Attrition of Knowledge Workforce in Healthcare in Northern parts of India–Health Information Technology as a Plausible Retention Strategy. *Bharati Vidyapeeth's Institute of Computer Applications and Management (BVICAM),* 411.

Bonias, D., Bartram, T., Leggat, S. G., & Stanton, P. (2010). Does psychological empowerment mediate the relationship between high performance work systems and patient care quality in hospitals? *Asia Pacific Journal of Human Resources, 48*(3), 319–337.

Boselie, P. (2010). High performance work practices in the health care sector: A Dutch case study. *International Journal of Manpower, 31*(1), 42–58.

Bothma, C. F., & Roodt, G. (2013). The validation of the turnover intention scale. *SA Journal of Human Resource Management, 11*(1), 1–12.

Collini, S. A., Guidroz, A. M., & Perez, L. M. (2015). Turnover in health care: The mediating effects of employee engagement. *Journal of Nursing Management, 23*(2), 169–178.

Danayiyen, A., & Bekaroglu, S. B. (2020). Development of The High-Performance Work Systems Scale for Hospitals: Validity and Reliability Study. *Research Journal of Business and Management, 7*(3), 128–138.

Dasgupta, P. (2014). Nurses' intention to leave: A qualitative study in private hospitals. *Globsyn Management Journal, 8*(1/2), 77.

Delery, J. E., & Doty, D. H. (1996). Modes of theorizing in strategic human resource management: Tests of universalistic, contingency, and configurational performance predictions. *Academy of Management Journal, 39*(4), 802–835. https://doi.org/10.2307/256713

Fahim, M. G. A. (2018). Strategic human resource management and public employee retention. *Review of Economics and Political Science, 3*(2), 20–39.

Fan, D., Cui, L., Zhang, M. M., Zhu, C. J., Härtel, C. E., & Nyland, C. (2014). Influence of high performance work systems on employee subjective well-being and job burnout: Empirical evidence from the Chinese healthcare sector. *The International Journal of Human Resource Management, 25*(7), 931–950.

Ghosh, P., Satyawadi, R., Prasad Joshi, J., & Shadman, M. (2013). Who stays with you? Factors predicting employees' intention to stay. *International Journal of Organizational Analysis, 21*(3), 288–312.

Grover, S., Sahoo, S., Bhalla, A., & Avasthi, A. (2018). Psychological problems and burnout among medical professionals of a tertiary care hospital of North India: A cross-sectional study. *Indian Journal of Psychiatry, 60*(2), 175. https://doi.org/10.4103/psychiatry.IndianJPsychiatry_254_17

Haines III, V. Y., Jalette, P., & Larose, K. (2010). The influence of human resource management practices on employee voluntary turnover rates in the Canadian non governmental sector. *ILR Review, 63*(2), 228–246.

Hiltrop, J.-M. (1999). The quest for the best: Human resource practices to attract and retain talent. *European Management Journal, 17*(4), 422–430.

Hogan, P., Moxham, L., & Dwyer, T. (2007). Human resource management strategies for the retention of nurses in acute care settings in hospitals in Australia. *Contemporary Nurse, 24*(2), 189–199.

Huselid, M. A. (1995). The impact of human resource management practices on turnover, productivity, and corporate financial performance. *Academy of Management Journal, 38*(3), 635–672.

Kloutsiniotis, P. V., & Mihail, D. M. (2019, November 27). HPWS: A Bundling or a Systems Approach? Evidence from the Greek Healthcare Sector. *Diamond Scientific Publishing.* Proceedings of The 2nd International Conference on Research in Business, Management and Economics. https://www.dpublication.com/abstract-of-2nd-icrbme/7029/

Leggat, S. G., Bartram, T., & Stanton, P. (2011). High performance work systems: The gap between policy and practice in health care reform. *Journal of Health Organization and Management, 25*(3), 281–297.

Mahmoud, G., & El-Sayed, N. (2016). High Performance Work Systems that Promote Nurses' Job Performance at Main Mansoura University Hospital. *Public Policy and Administration Research, 6*(9), 59–67.

Martín-Alcázar, F., Romero-Fernández, P. M., & Sánchez-Gardey, G. (2005). Strategic human resource management: Integrating the universalistic, contingent, configurational and contextual perspectives. *The International Journal of Human Resource Management, 16*(5), 633–659. https://doi.org/10.1080/09585190500082519

Meyer, J. P., Allen, N. J., & Gellatly, I. R. (1990). Affective and continuance commitment to the organization: Evaluation of measures and analysis of concurrent and time-lagged relations. *Journal of Applied Psychology, 75*(6), 710–720. https://doi.org/10.1037/0021-9010.75.6.710

Mohd Nasurdin, A., Tan, C. L., & Naseer Khan, S. (2020). Can high performance work practices and satisfaction predict job performance? An examination of the Malaysian private health-care sector. *International Journal of Quality and Service Sciences, 12*(4), 521–540.

Nasiru, M., & Kwabe, U. D. (2020). Effect of High-Performance Work Practices on Organizational Performance of General Hospital, Mubi, Adamawa State, Nigeria. *International Journal of Innovative Research and Development.*

Omanwar, S. P., & Agrawal, R. K. (2021). Servant leadership, organizational identification and turnover intention: An empirical study in hospitals. *International Journal of Organizational Analysis, 30*(2), 239–258. https://doi.org/10.1108/IJOA-08-2020-2374

Pfeffer, J. (1998). Seven Practices of Successful Organizations | Semantic Scholar. *CALIFORNIA MANAGEMENT REVIEW, 40*(2), 96–124.

Pittino, D., Visintin, F., Lenger, T., & Sternad, D. (2016). Are high performance work practices really necessary in family SMEs? An analysis of the impact on employee retention. *Journal of Family Business Strategy, 7*(2), 75–89.

Qureshi, T. M. (2019). Talent retention using high performance work systems. *International Journal of Organizational Innovation, 12*(2).

Rani, R., & Gandotra, R. (2015). The impact of bundled high performance human resource practices on intention to leave. *The International Journal of Educational Management, 29*(4), 431–460.

Rubel, M. R. B., Hung Kee, D. M., & Rimi, N. N. (2021). High-performance work practices and medical professionals' work outcomes: The mediating effect of perceived organizational support. *Journal of Advances in Management Research, 18*(3), 368–391.

Schuler, R. S., Jackson, S. E., & Storey, J. (2001). *HRM and its link with strategic management* (J. Storey, Ed.). Thomson Learning EMEA. http://hed.thomsonlearning.co.uk/instructors/product.aspx?isbn=1861526059

Scotti, D. J., Harmon, J., & Behson, S. J. (2007). Links among high-performance work environment, service quality, and customer satisfaction: An extension to the healthcare sector. *Journal of Healthcare Management, 52*(2), 109–124.

Semedo, C. (2017). *The Wiley Blackwell Handbook of the Psychology of Recruitment, Selection and Employee Retention.*

Siyal, S., Xin, C., Peng, X., Siyal, A. W., & Ahmed, W. (2020). Why do high-performance human resource practices matter for employee outcomes in public sector universities? The mediating role of person–organization fit mechanism. *Sage Open, 10*(3), 2158244020947424.

Syed, Z., & Jamal, W. (n.d.). *Universalistic Perspective of HRM and Organisational Performance: Meta-Analytical Study.*

Tharenou, P., Saks, A. M., & Moore, C. (2007). A review and critique of research on training and organizational-level outcomes. *Human Resource Management Review, 17*(3), 251–273. https://doi.org/10.1016/j.hrmr.2007.07.004

Tzafrir, S. S. (2006). A universalistic perspective for explaining the relationship between HRM practices and firm performance at different points in time. *Journal of Managerial Psychology, 21*(2), 109–130. https://doi.org/10.1108/02683940610650730

World Health Organization, Anand, S., & Fan, V. (2016). *The health workforce in India.* World Health Organization. https://iris.who.int/handle/10665/250369

Zurn, P., Dolea, C., & Stilwell, B. (2005). *Nurse retention and recruitment: Developing a motivated workforce.* International Council of Nurses.

www.ingramcontent.com/pod-product-compliance
Lightning Source LLC
Chambersburg PA
CBHW041645150726
48005CB00015BA/2320